Integrative Nutrition

CASE HISTORIES
the dynamic future of nutrition

ISBN 0-9773025-3-9

Published by Integrative Nutrition Publishing, Inc.
3 East 28 Street
New York, NY 10016
www.integrativenutrition.com

Printed on recycled paper.

Acknowledgments

Special thanks to:

Joshua Rosenthal
for primary food, deconstructing cravings and the magic of mirroring

Tricia Napor
for her dedicated guidance of Integrative Nutrition Publishing

Jen Rosenblum
for bringing this book to life with passion and intelligence

Caryn Fishlevich and Erika Tsoukanelis
for their thoughtful insights and endless support

Integrative Nutrition Staff
for going above and beyond every day

Integrative Nutrition Students
for keeping us moving forward with your desire to learn and grow

Integrative Nutrition Alumni
for propelling our mission to improve the health and happiness of people around the world

Table of Contents

Introduction

by Joshua Rosenthal

This is a book about transformation. You are about to meet a group of amazing, talented people who have been forever changed by the simple, yet profound recipe for living that we teach here at Integrative Nutrition.

Understand, we have a vision. We foresee a brilliant future in which the people of this world live in balance: taking in wholesome food, finding pleasure in what they do, reveling in their own physicality, communicating and growing in their relationships, and engaging in deep spiritual practice. The current health crisis—with its epidemics of obesity, heart disease, diabetes and cancer—will be resolved. No longer will doctors rely on expensive medications and risky operations to fix what is wrong. Instead, healthcare will focus on education, prevention and empowerment of the individual. People will come to trust the wisdom of their own bodies. They will recognize the plain power of sleep, water, clean food and movement to keep them aglow with health and vitality.

Neither corporations nor government will facilitate this revolution. Outward change always begins within the individual's heart and mind. And when that individual comes together with others, when a unified, dedicated group of like-minded souls works toward a common goal, that is when a force for social change is created. It is such a force that will bring our vision into being.

The graduates profiled in this book are the new leaders creating the dynamic future of nutrition. During our training, they underwent significant improvements in their health and lives, and these changes opened them further to their own depths. They are all unique, wise people, worthy of trust who want to make a difference, and through our unique education on nutritional theory and balanced living, they became highly effective in the science and art of creating personal transformation in the lives of clients, family, friends and anyone they meet. When an open, willing person hires a certified health counselor, they learn to live and eat in ways that bring passion to every single day of their lives. Such receptive people share their stories in this book as well. They had access to the best doctors, hospitals and medications, but it was not until their work with one of our graduates that they experienced true breakthroughs in their health.

I hope that you see yourself in these chronicles of healing, and grow inspired by the tremendous achievements of these people. Be assured that you possess the same inherent capacity for success, health and happiness. Together, we will manifest the vibrant future we all deserve.

Medical Doctors

There is no question that modern medicine is astounding in its lifesaving feats. If a heart or liver weakens or fails, a new one can take its place. If a limb is severed, it may be reattached. Cancers are eradicated and complex surgeries performed through the smallest incisions. And there are more breakthroughs every day, with stem cell and other research promising bright advances. Yet there is a distressing incongruity in today's healthcare system. While technology has skyrocketed, so have the costs of care. There are many who carry no health insurance. Bankruptcies caused by impossible medical bills are common. Well-meaning physicians have no choice but to prolong wait times and shorten visits with patients, and liability insurance and medical school bills are putting some of these doctors out of business. Other physicians have allowed themselves to be regarded as all-knowing, encouraging patients to bow to them and rarely taking the time to understand an individual's needs. They fail to be open to new ways of healing that could greatly benefit their patients, including alternatives that involve the crucial role of nutrition in health.

Thankfully, there are some extraordinary physicians seeking change. They are responding to their patients' interest in nutrition and prevention, while resisting the trend to treat all ailments with expensive medications and operations. These doctors, who recognize that diet and lifestyle changes significantly improve the health of their patients, are wildly successful and in high demand. Integrative Nutrition is proud to say that a number of these physicians have been students at our school. They were led to us by an earnest desire to offer comprehensive protocols that incorporate whole food nutrition, balanced lifestyle and loving self-care. The doctors you will read about in this chapter are among those breaking way for a new paradigm in medicine. They have come to understand the importance of gathering complete health histories from patients, and they engage their patients in dialogue, rather than monopolizing the conversation.

Imagine if every doctor in America had a thorough education in nutrition as the foundation of health. Picture a physician who provides a deep level of care that includes not just abstract medical knowledge, but insight into your personal health concerns and goals. This is the medical model that Integrative Nutrition is working toward. It is our mission to heal the healthcare system one doctor and one patient at a time.

Karlene ChinQuee
MD, FACOG

Class of 2006 | New York, NY

It's a great life if you don't weaken. —John Buchan

Job: board certified obstetrician, gynecologist and surgeon
Childhood dream: to be an interpretive modern dancer or physician
Favorite snack food: grapefruit, berries, almonds, cashews or pistachios
Favorite healthy food: salmon, broccoli or carrots
Favorite nutrition book: *The South Beach Diet* by Arthur Agaston, MD
Favorite exercise: weight lifting
Favorite activity outside of work: attending cultural events—operas, plays, musicals, dance performances, jazz concerts and art exhibits
Favorite vacation spot: St. Bart's, French West Indies
Craziest thing I've ever done: learned to windsurf and water-ski when I couldn't swim
Wildest dream: to continue to globally expand Heartbeats of the World, Inc., my nonprofit humanitarian organization to help women and children in underserved areas of the world
Proudest moment: when my grandmother made her first trip outside of Jamaica at age 82 to attend my graduation from medical school
Biggest challenge: not knowing how to say no to someone in need
Nutrition education is important because: good nutrition is one of the most important factors in maintaining good health.
What I love about health counseling: being able to guide and empower my patients to be partners in their own healthcare
What I love about Integrative Nutrition: They teach that there must be a balance in mind, body and spirit in order to achieve optimum health.
What I love about my star client, Catherine: her strong desire to be healthy. She asks very good questions and works with me in a team approach to achieve better health.

ABOUT MY PRACTICE

Ideal Balance, LLC | www.idealbalance.org

My medical specialty is: women's health issues. The health concerns I deal with most often are gynecological and pap smear exams, hormonal and menstrual imbalance, birth control, holistic fertility support, uterine fibroids, polycystic ovaries, PMS, HPV, endometriosis, weight, stress, natural treatments for menopause, and osteoporosis.

My typical client is: a highly intelligent, highly accomplished professional or executive who is overstressed and wants to find balance in her life.

I chose to continue my education at Integrative Nutrition because: I was fascinated by their concept of "reshaping the health of America." I liked the idea of being educated on the many dietary perspectives, and I was pleased that their guest faculty includes best-known authors and speakers in the nutrition field. Another draw for me was the business organization part of the curriculum.

Integrative Nutrition has enhanced my ability to provide quality healthcare by: showing me where I need to put my focus. Patients come to me from different parts of the world because they know I will spend time with them and that I genuinely care about them. In school I learned to set boundaries and to formally structure my time with clients so that I honor myself, my time and my services. The six-month program is a perfect framework for me. I use the basic structure the school teaches, then add more of what I have to offer as a physician, such as blood work and natural hormone therapies.

The top three results my clients get from working with me are: They feel better about themselves and feel assured that they are receiving the highest level of professional care. They also feel well-informed, special and genuinely cared for.

In addition to seeing clients and patients, I also: am founder, president and CEO of a nonprofit organization, Heartbeats of the World, Inc. We provide medical resources and education addressing the prevention and treatment of HIV/AIDS, sexually transmitted diseases, teen pregnancy and unemployment. We have established six schools on the island of Jamaica that provide education and vocational training to young people who have been left behind, and we are developing more outreach initiatives in Harlem and the Bronx. Heartbeats of the World was inspired by my spiritual belief that we are all one, and motivated by a love of humanity.

What I love about what I do: OB/GYN is a "happy specialty." The journey with a mom though her prenatal care, which culminates in a healthy mommy/healthy baby is a very special treat for me. While delivering babies and doing gynecological surgery is an important aspect, the specialty of OB/GYN allows me the privilege of creating an integrative medical practice that combines the best of conventional medicine with natural therapies. I am truly blessed to be able to work with a diverse group of women patients who are exceptional, intelligent and highly accomplished, and who are willing to be partners in their care and who teach me so much.

My greatest success so far: has been establishing a solo practitioner's medical practice in New York City and maintaining that practice through the referrals of satisfied patients.

In the future, I see myself: writing a book about health and wellness and expanding my integrated medical and health practice.

CLIENT TESTIMONIAL

Catherine

32 | law firm assistant manager | New York, NY

I work hard at my law firm and take care of my sweet seven-year-old daughter. I also have endometriosis. The back of my uterus is attached to my intestines by lesions which causes a lot of pain at certain times of the month. For a long time doctors couldn't tell me what was going on. Everyone had different opinions. Some said there was nothing wrong with me. Some said they wanted to do surgery. Finally I was referred to Dr. ChinQuee, and she figured it out.

Dr. ChinQuee is not your typical doctor. At first I was shocked by how thorough she is. She made me feel comfortable and welcome. She went through all my diagnoses, procedures and treatments so I would understand them. With her, wellness is a balance between medical health and one's personal life. I tend to take on too much, and she helped me to see how that would affect me physically. I saw that stress contributes to the pain. She taught me that it's important to sleep, to say no and to take care of myself. I learned how to maintain personal balance, what vitamins to take and how to eat to nourish my uterus and ovaries.

When I first came to Dr. ChinQuee I was in extreme pain. After being her patient, my pain is at a manageable level. I've become more conscious of what triggers it and how to avoid or reduce it. I take more responsibility now and that makes a big difference. Dr. ChinQuee is a very trustworthy, warm and caring person. I tell her I would walk from China to work with her because she's that good! Now that I have more energy and less pain, I'm looking forward to going back to school and to spending more time with my daughter.

Doug Miller
MD

Class of 2005 | Cromwell, CT

An optimist is a person who sees a green light everywhere, while a pessimist sees only the red stoplight. The truly wise person is color-blind.
                                        —Albert Schweitzer

Job: gastroenterologist
Childhood ambition: to build skyscrapers
Favorite snack food: medjool dates
Favorite healthy food: fermented sauerkraut
Favorite nutrition book: *Eat, Drink, and Be Healthy* by Walter Willet, MD
Favorite exercise: cycling
Favorite activity outside of work: cooking for friends and family
What I do to treat myself: eat a piece of really good dark chocolate
What I do to feel at peace: hike to the top of Mount Mansfield in Vermont
Wildest dream: to scuba dive the Great Barrier Reef
Proudest moment: my son winning an award for best young playwright
in Connecticut
Biggest challenge: finding balance in my life
Health concerns I've cleared up: abnormal cholesterol levels
Nutrition education is important because: food is medicine but rarely prescribed.
What I love about Integrative Nutrition: the comprehensive approach and
intelligent integration of primary foods
What I love about my star client, Andrea: everything I learned from her

ABOUT MY PRACTICE

Digestive Health Specialists | dmiller@dhspecialists.com

My medical specialty is: gastroenterology, which includes treating common disorders like irritable bowel syndrome and acid reflux disease.

My typical patient: has minor digestive issues, wants to be reassured that there is nothing seriously wrong and craves understanding.

I chose to continue my education at Integrative Nutrition because: I was intrigued by their comprehensive approach and needed a vehicle to expand my approach to my patients. The nutrition training of most physicians is really lacking. I found that with being a conventional doctor I would reach a certain point with a patient and then have to say, "Sorry, that's all I can do. I just can't get you better." I wanted to go a step beyond that.

Integrative Nutrition has enhanced my ability to provide quality healthcare by: expanding my nutrition education and teaching me how to really listen to my patients. I talk much more with them about their eating habits and am much more tuned in to what's going on in their lives. I can hear what they are not telling me—that they really want more than a written prescription. They want to understand their disorders and learn lifestyle changes necessary to promote healing.

The top three results my patients get from working with me are: education, fresh ideas and durable results. They are very happy that someone is taking time and effort to explore their issues with them. It's unique in a doctor.

In addition to seeing patients, I also: am the past Chief of the Medical Staff at MidState Medical Center in Meriden, CT, and I am on the clinical faculty at the Yale School of Medicine.

What I love about what I do: having a positive impact on people's lives every day I go to work.

My greatest success so far: doing volunteer work at a medical clinic in the Dominican Republic. They are very proud of their hospital and are doing great work there. I saw patients in mobile villages of migrant workers. They had no healthcare, so the hospital brought healthcare to them. I got to go out to the villages and help immunize kids, treat hypertension and make sure they were getting proper nutrition. It was just a fabulous experience, and I plan to go back.

In the future, I see myself: continuing to broaden my knowledge of alternative approaches to gastrointestinal diseases, and integrating them into my practice.

CLIENT TESTIMONIAL

Andrea

66 | business owner | Cromwell, CT

I've had a great life. I've owned several businesses, including restaurants, furniture stores and a consulting practice. I have a wonderful family with my son, four grandchildren and two brothers. My greatest accomplishment has been raising my family to be good citizens of this world. I am also blessed with good physical health, but I developed a hormonal or chemical imbalance that was setting off panic and anxiety attacks. When I needed help, Dr. Miller came to my home and calmed me down. We discussed what to do to get control of my feelings and feel like myself again. He has been guiding me ever since that time. He really knows me and cares about me. I can discuss anything with him.

Before we started working together on my food, I tried to eat balanced meals, but I was able to make more healthy changes after working with him. Now I eat more whole grains, nuts, dried fruit and fish and omega oils. I've made changes in my breakfast, eating more whole grain breads and peanut butter. We also added many relaxation techniques to help with the anxiety, like guided imagery, deep breathing and getting massages and more exercise. In consultation with Dr. Miller I was able to get on the right medication in the right dosage for me.

These days I am feeling much better. My energy and anxiety levels have improved, and I've lost 10 pounds. I'm satisfied with my life and will continue to enjoy what I'm doing. Using a combination of wellness skills and medication seems to be the right path for me. Dr. Miller allows me that luxury of choosing what is best for me.

Nancy Weiss
MD

Class of 2005 | Eastchester, NY

What lies behind us and what lies before us are tiny matters compared to what lies within us.
— Ralph Waldo Emerson

Job: physician
Childhood ambition: to find Prince Charming
Favorite snack food: dark-chocolate–covered almonds
Favorite healthy food: grapes or mangos
Favorite nutrition book: *The China Study* by T. Colin Campbell, PhD
Favorite exercise: tai chi or yoga
Favorite activity outside of work: golf
What I do to treat myself: Angel Feet reflexology treatment or lunch with a good friend
What I do to feel at peace: take my dog for a long walk
Wildest dream: to fully realize myself as a spiritual being in the present moment
Proudest moment: graduating from medical school
Biggest challenge: going to medical school
Health concerns I've cleared up: low energy, constipation
Nutrition education is important because: what we eat becomes part of us and therefore has the power to affect us in so many ways.
What I love about Integrative Nutrition: It teaches you to extract information from multiple sources and integrate it into a whole that resonates with the uniqueness of each person.
What I love about my star client, Joyce: her positive attitude, courage, creativity and willingness to try new things

ABOUT MY PRACTICE

Weiss Wellness | 914.420.6477

My medical specialty is: internal medicine (treatment and general care of adult patients).

My typical patient is: "stuck" in their life and wants to eat healthier, have more energy, lose weight, be happier and adopt a healthier lifestyle.

I chose to continue my education at Integrative Nutrition because: I am a seeker of alternative treatments, and I wanted to deepen my skills and practice. I got the Integrative Nutrition catalog in the mail and found it inspiring. I wasn't interested in going to a nutrition school, but I loved this school's philosophy.

Integrative Nutrition has enhanced my ability to provide quality healthcare by: broadening my knowledge of nutrition and how it affects us as individuals, and by helping me understand that "nutrition" is not just the food we eat, but the quality of our work, relationships, spiritual practice, etc. In my medical practice I don't have time to do anything extensive with my patients on nutrition. It is not as effective as a counseling program. If I see a patient who needs help with their diet, they become my health counseling client outside of the practice.

The top three results my clients get from working with me are: eliminating physical health problems, following a healthier diet, and identifying and improving areas of stress and limitation in their lives.

In addition to seeing patients and clients, I also: play golf, read, practice yoga and tai chi, and spend lots of time with my husband, family, friends and my dog Casey.

What I love about what I do: As a doctor I have the privilege of working with people in a way that most people don't. People bring me their problems and let me into their lives. It's an opportunity to really listen to people and help them understand what their obstacles are, and then guide them. It is always a shared experience, as helpful for me as it is for them. I love the personal connection. I feel I am really making a lasting contribution to someone's life.

My greatest success so far: I had a patient with pruritis—total body itching. As his doctor, I gave him all sorts of tests and could never figure it out. Then the patient asked to participate in my group health counseling program. He participated enthusiastically, transforming his diet, losing weight and creating abundant energy and well-being in his life. He is now totally cured of the body itching. I love telling this story. Where I failed as a doctor, I succeeded as a health counselor.

In the future, I see myself: continuing to develop both my medical and health counseling practices so I can provide more for my patients, and creating a lifestyle that affords me freedom to pursue all the things I enjoy doing.

CLIENT TESTIMONIAL

Joyce

63 | housewife | Staten Island, NY

I'm a native New Yorker with a great family. I love my kids and grandkids. I'm really into cooking. I'll make just about anything, and I enjoy improving on my recipes. I had been going from doctor to doctor because these weird pains were waking me up at night. The doctors put me through all kinds of tests, but couldn't figure out what was wrong. They would tell me to relax, lighten up and try some yoga. That wasn't enough for me. My doctor's office referred me to Nancy. She figured out that there wasn't anything major wrong with me and offered to spend more time with me to help solve the problem. I signed up for a six-month nutrition program with her.

Nancy helped me a lot. By getting to know me inside and out, she helped me discover that I have an especially sensitive body. I have to respect it and be aware. I react strongly to everything, so I have to figure out myself what foods I can tolerate or not. Nancy helped me to understand the body I'm living with and that made it easier. She also got me eating new foods like quinoa, sea vegetables, spelt cereal and different greens.

Today my pains have eased and I'm sleeping better. Breathing deeply, relaxing and eating the right foods really helps. Nancy is an excellent doctor. She answered all my questions and made me feel comfortable. She's not quick to give out medicine unless you really need it, and she's always there to help. She's the way a doctor should be.

2

Healthcare Professionals

The students at our school are natural healers. They are sensitive, caring individuals who listen intently to others, who empathize deeply with those around them and who want to help. People feel drawn to them and often open up to them. They come to Integrative Nutrition with inherent abilities to facilitate transformative healing for their friends, family and future clients.

Some students are already in helping professions. They have found contentment as nurses, physical therapists, dentists, registered dieticians and psychiatrists. Over the years, clients have come to them seeking guidance on nutrition. They have either felt empty-handed or responded with free advice, and now they aspire to fill in the gaps. Integrative Nutrition floods them with knowledge. They learn about nutritional theory, listen to world-renowned experts and experiment with their own diets in order to increase what they have to offer their patients.

The dedicated graduates profiled in this chapter have been empowered by our training to become stronger, wiser healthcare professionals. They examine what their clients are eating. They work with them around building healthy relationships, resolving career issues and fortifying spiritual practices. As a result, their clients' health concerns subside more quickly and completely than ever before. By adding health counseling to their repertoire, these already successful health professionals become highly sought after and create sensational businesses. Recognizing them as the amazing healers they are, Integrative Nutrition supports them to dramatically evolve in their lives, both personally and professionally.

Lynn Goldstein
MS, RD, CDN

Class of 2006 | New York, NY

To eat is a necessity but to eat intelligently is an art.

— François de La Rochefoucauld

Job: registered dietician

Childhood ambition: to be a lawyer

Favorite snack food: Snyder's salted waffle pretzels

Favorite healthy food: raspberries

Favorite nutrition book: *Healing with Whole Foods* by Paul Pitchford

Favorite exercise: power yoga

Favorite activity outside of work: walking my dog

What I do to treat myself: massage, facial or manicure-pedicure

What I do to feel at peace: play with my dog in the park, take a yoga class or spend an evening with friends or family

Wildest dream: to prevent all cancers with nutrition

Proudest moment: I recently had a patient tell me that I saved her life. It doesn't get much better than that.

Biggest challenge: trusting myself enough to succeed in what I am doing

Health concerns I've cleared up: depression, acne and overweight

Nutrition education is important because: it provides scientific background and knowledge on how food works in the body. It has taught me how food relates to many different disease states, which allows me to work with a broad array of patients.

What I love about Integrative Nutrition: This course taught me everything my masters program was lacking. It was about being proactive with nutrition, not reactive, which I think is such a big problem in our country, where medical people are taught only how to heal people once they are sick, and not before.

What I love about my star client, Martha: No matter what she was going through, she would come in with a smile on her face. She was always willing to listen and trust.

ABOUT MY PRACTICE

You Are What You Eat | lgoldre@hotmail.com | www.youarewhatyoueat.com

My medical specialty is: cancer prevention and treatment, gastrointestinal disorders and general disease prevention. You Are What You Eat is a nutrition program that focuses on individual needs to improve health. I believe that food is the center of our world, and it makes up who we are from the inside out.

My typical client is: almost anyone. I work with men and women, young and old. The clients who touch me the most are those who are willing to listen, learn and trust long enough to make changes in their lives.

I chose to continue my education at Integrative Nutrition because: although my masters in clinical nutrition taught me many things about helping people get healthier, it taught only one way of doing things. No one way works for everyone. My education was limiting in that it taught how to work with a disease, not a person. I was lacking that ability to really connect and listen to my patients. Being an RD is something I love and am very proud of, but because of Integrative Nutrition I have become a more well-rounded educator.

Integrative Nutrition has enhanced my ability to provide quality healthcare by: teaching me how to give diet and lifestyle recommendations based on what a patient needs, and not what a textbook says. I utilize all diet theories, both from Eastern and Western philosophies, to come up with the perfect solution for my patients. I have learned to listen and give a supportive hand, which makes patients feel they are really cared for. That is priceless.

The top three results my clients get from working with me are: weight loss, stress reduction and improvement in whatever GI disorder or cancer therapy side effects they are dealing with.

In addition to one-on-one counseling, I also: work for an outpatient clinic called The Jay Monahan Center for Gastrointestinal Health.

What I love about what I do: helping people improve their lives. When my clients leave me they are usually smiling, and they thank me for helping them. I don't think you can get anything better than that from a job. I also love working in a field that allows me to help myself at the same time as I help others. No one is without need of nutritional guidance.

My greatest success so far has been: doing a TV interview on *Business Week* discussing organic foods, and having the opportunity to work at The Jay Monahan Center.

In the future, I see myself: continuing my current work, opening a wellness center in New York City, and traveling and giving lectures on living healthy.

CLIENT TESTIMONIAL

Martha

65 | retired | New York, NY

I'm married and retired, and I've lived in the city for many years. I enjoy being active—playing sports, reading and hiking. However, I have colitis, which was slowing me down. I needed to see somebody about it. I didn't think I had a bad diet, but the food I was eating was affecting my stomach. My doctor referred me to Lynn. She really knows a lot about food and was very helpful in terms of figuring out what to eat and how to enjoy food again. She got me interested in cooking and got me to try different foods I had never really thought of before. My new favorite foods include a lot more cooked vegetables. Also, baked fruit was something I would have never thought of, and it is delicious.

I was able to talk to Lynn about a lot of areas of my life. She helped me to stop rushing through my meals, to pay attention and enjoy my food. She also recommended yoga, hot baths and helpful teas. She always had good ideas for me. I've slowly gotten better. My digestion has quieted down and gotten much better. I have less pain. I know these changes are connected with my diet. It makes a huge difference. Things in my life are definitely better. My mood and energy level are higher, and I'm able to do more activities.

Lynn's got a wonderful personality. She's very encouraging and not wedded to one particular way of doing something. She's very creative in her approach, willing to look at what works and what doesn't. The best thing about her is her positive, upbeat approach to everything. She really believes in what she teaches.

Mary N. Joyce
RN

Class of 2004 | Queens, NY

Don't sweat the small stuff, and it's all small stuff. – Richard Carlson

Job: public health registered nurse
Childhood ambition: to discover the hidden secrets of the universe
Favorite snack food: dark chocolate or salt and pepper Kettle chips
Favorite healthy food: roasted kale and spirulina balls
Favorite nutrition book: *Healthy Life Kitchen* by Marilu Henner
Favorite exercise: walking or jogging
Favorite activity outside of work: eating and entertaining
What I do to treat myself: create "time-outs"
What I do to feel at peace: quiet my mind
Wildest dream: to sail down the Amazon River
Proudest moment: when my daughter told a friend, "My mom doesn't use medicine. We use food and herbs to stay healthy. They taste good and are better for you."
Biggest challenge: being still
Health concerns I've cleared up: sugar cravings and digestive issues
What I love about Integrative Nutrition: how they create community
Nutrition education is important because: it is the foundation stone of all health and healing.
What I love about being a health counselor: discovering each person's true essence
What I love about my star client, Sylvie: her delight at the changes she experienced

ABOUT MY PRACTICE

Health From Within Us | mary@healthfromwithin.us | www.healthfromwithin.us

My counseling specialty is: teaching health and healing through nutrition. I have individual holistic health clients, work as a school nurse and work part-time in a radiologist's office as a nurse. Many of the patients there have cancer. I speak with everyone about their diet and how they can keep themselves nourished and healthy. I refer many patients to healthy resources, such as nutrition books or cooking classes.

My typical client is: an adult or adolescent who wants to eat better, feel healthier and lose weight. Many of the adults are stressed-out perfectionists.

I chose to continue my education at Integrative Nutrition because: when I trained as a nurse in the '80s, nursing was a holistic practice, addressing the whole person—mind, body, soul and family. Then nursing became more corporate and disease-focused, like other aspects of the medical industry. I heard about Integrative Nutrition years ago and knew I wanted to go. It is the grassroots center for healing through food and nutrition. Incorporating holistic health counseling makes me a much better nurse. I don't even separate the ideas of nursing and holistic counseling in my mind anymore. Instead I focus on integrating all of my practices and experience.

Integrative Nutrition has enhanced my ability to provide quality healthcare by: giving me the tools to combine my nursing knowledge with holistic counseling. I initiate healthy lifestyle changes for every patient I meet, even if I am with them for only a few minutes.

The top three results my clients get from working with me are: weight loss, decreased sugar cravings and shedding guilty feelings about food. Many say that working with me helps them feel grounded, more in touch with themselves and their bodies. I help them reduce stress and channel their perfectionism towards projects that bring them pleasure. When we find something fun or healthy for them to focus on, they experience positive changes very quickly.

What I love about what I do: touching my patients' lives and being personal with them. In my work I demonstrate that a holistic approach is positive and that it works. This really is the way to health. All paths are leading to the holistic health approach, with nutrition as the foundation.

In addition to one-on-one counseling, I also: teach fun workshops and classes, provide herbal and Bach flower essence therapies, and offer Reiki and craniosacral treatments.

My greatest success so far: is any major health victory for my clients. For example, one went off diet soda and lost five pounds within a week. Another got off of hypertension medication through healthier eating and lifestyle changes. My training in holistic counseling has enhanced my nursing skills, and my patients feel the benefits.

In the future, I see myself: creating a sliding scale holistic clinic to make holistic services available to the entire population. My time at Integrative Nutrition supported and developed my belief that modern medical practice needs to shift away from a disease orientation. Some institutions are changing and becoming more open, which is great, but I believe that more hospitals and hospices need to take a more holistic approach. I'm someone who is going to help to change this system.

CLIENT TESTIMONIAL

Sylvie

52 | midwife | Valley Cottage, NY

I've been a midwife for 18 years and now own my own practice. I'm passionate about women's health. Years ago I delivered Mary's wonderful baby girl, and we stayed in touch. When she became interested in holistic health and healing, I decided to hire her. I was in a very stressful time in my life. I was working around the clock, living on diet soda all night to stay awake. My blood pressure and cholesterol were high. I'd stopped exercising and was on Lipitor and blood pressure medication. As a health care provider myself, I knew I was making poor choices.

Mary enabled me to reach goals that were doable within my hectic life. She encouraged me to hire help for my business so I could get more sleep. I stopped drinking soda, cut back on coffee, reduced eggs and ate more vegetables. I started exercising again, lost 15 pounds, and even ran two half-marathons. Mary helped me get off all the medications in just six months, which was really great. The last thing I wanted was to be on medication for the rest of my life.

Mary was especially good at helping me set realistic goals, like substituting or reducing. It's not all or nothing. Being expected to be perfect never works, and Mary has a real sense of that. She's such a wonderful person. I really benefited from spending time with her.

Dara Kessler
DDS

Class of 2003 | New York, NY

To be or not to be is a question of compromise. Either you be or you don't be.

– Golda Meir

Job: holistic dentist
Childhood ambition: to be self-sufficient
Favorite snack food: Tostitos chips with homemade guacamole
Favorite healthy food: wilted chard with savory tahini sauce
Favorite nutrition book: *Eating Well for Optimum Health* by Andrew Weil, MD
Favorite type of exercise: swimming or playing tennis
Favorite activity outside of work: playing with my son
Favorite vacation spot: Hawaii
What I do to feel at peace: attend festive Friday night services at my shul
Wildest dream: to spend more time traveling than working
Proudest moment: becoming a mom
Biggest challenge: maintaining a balanced life in Manhattan
Health concerns I've cleared up: skin problems
Nutrition education is important because: it empowers you to take responsibility for your own health.
What I love about Integrative Nutrition: exploring all the different dietary options
What I love about my star client, Joshua: his openness

ABOUT MY PRACTICE

The Integrative Dental Practice of New York | doctordara@yahoo.com

My medical specialty is: general dentistry. Over the years I have studied and adopted a more integrated approach. I joined a practice with other holistic dentists where we introduce patients to homeopathy, acupuncture and nutrition to help them with their oral health.

My typical patient is: almost anyone. Many are holistically oriented and mindful of their diets. I also work with patients who are chemically sensitive, who are very ill or who are recovering from major diseases. They want a dentist who understands and supports them and who can talk about the importance of nutrition. They like that I am familiar with natural approaches to health and that I am selective about what dental materials I use.

I chose to continue my health education at Integrative Nutrition because: I was interested in studying nutrition, and I loved the curriculum they offered. There is no training for holistic dentists, so the school gave me my training in a holistic approach. In addition, the schedule was very practical.

Integrative Nutrition has enhanced my ability to provide quality healthcare by: exposing me to many different dietary theories. The school enhanced my nutrition knowledge and grounded it in great listening, teaching and counseling skills. As a counselor I am able to do a lot of patient education and help clients change their lifestyles. I also really learned to take care of myself!

The top three results my patients get from working with me are: healthy teeth, healthy gums and the ability to maintain them! Another big benefit is leaving my office knowing how to take care of themselves as whole people. People are pleasantly surprised that they come in to talk about teeth and end up talking about their kids, their feelings or their work-life balance. It's all interconnected, and most people are starved for this kind of support.

In addition to seeing patients, I also: am a wife and mom. I spend most of my time raising my one-year-old son (and cooking him healthy, homemade food). I am also active with The Shul of New York. I try to stay fit, so I exercise regularly.

What I love about what I do: getting my patients engaged in their own health and teaching them how to take care of themselves. I also love the flexibility that this career provides. Health counseling is my way of manifesting what I think of as our basic rights. It is our right to know how our bodies work and how to take care of them, how to feed ourselves or how to have a balanced life. This is my way of helping the world make more sense.

My greatest success so far has been: making the transition to being a working mom.

In the future, I see myself: working with my partners to expand our dental practice, which will create all sorts of possibilities!

CLIENT TESTIMONIAL

Joshua

36 | craniosacral therapist | New York, NY

I love my work. I help people with jaw grinding, migraines, back pain and other issues. I'm suited for and committed to this job, as well as my community, spirituality and home life. I first came to Dara with a negative association between dentists and pain because I'd had about two cavities a year since I was a kid, and I have lots of fillings. I needed to establish a trusting relationship with a dentist before I could take their advice. I value Dara for being a safe dentist who I can relate to. She is interested in me as a whole person. She has a professional, caring touch, and I like how she explains how my choices impact my health, instead of lecturing me in a parental way about what I should be doing differently.

Dara was able to show me that my tooth deterioration was related to my acidic diet. She recommended a more alkalinizing diet, and brushing in the morning with baking soda. Now I've taken all wheat out of my diet, I eat a lot more greens and I've let go of using sugar. I've stopped snacking in the middle of the night and I chew my food more. I came to understand that in my old diet I had been using food to manage my mood.

My oral health has definitely gotten better. The deterioration has stopped. I've had only two cavities in the last few years, instead of at every visit. Because of the diet changes, I'm a lot calmer and more present. I feel very energized, which has helped me to build my business. Dara created a safe environment in which I could make changes to my entire health as well as my teeth.

3

Speaking Out

Throughout history, individuals such as Mahatma Gandhi, Martin Luther King, Jr. and Susan B. Anthony triumphed by going against the grain. In the face of huge odds, they used their voices to fight oppression and promote freedom.

Today, we need leaders to confront the mayhem happening around nutrition and health. Obesity, heart disease, diabetes and other food-related illnesses are affecting the lives of millions of Americans and beginning to spread around the world at alarming rates. There is an unfortunate lack of advice and education about the simplicity and effectiveness of adopting a healthy lifestyle. Instead, the public gets complicated nutrition advice from biased sources such as diet books, politicians and talk show hosts. The world needs to hear from smart, concerned people who speak the truth simply because they care.

Students at Integrative Nutrition are intelligent, passionate, articulate people who, for whatever reason, learned to stay quiet. They have vast knowledge about health, nutrition and the human condition. To encourage our students to become elements of change in society, we cultivate their ability to speak up. In addition to nutrition theory, we teach confidence, self-esteem and public speaking. Upon graduation, our students have an enormous amount of confidence and floor the people they meet with their eloquence.

We are not simply a nutrition school; we are a movement. We are dedicated to the belief that the world can be a happy, healthy place. It is through the bravery of the individuals who are standing up, speaking out and working with the public around the crucial matters of health and nutrition that this country, and the world at large, will see an improved healthcare system supporting each person's right to live a healthy life.

Teresa Kay-Aba Kennedy

Class of 2003 | Harlem, NY

For God has not given us a spirit of fear; but of power and love, and of wisdom. -The Bible

Job before Integrative Nutrition: vice president of business operations at MTV Networks
Childhood ambition: to be a painter or entertainment lawyer
Favorite snack food: blueberry yo-goat (yogurt from goat's milk)
Favorite healthy food: kale chili with brown rice
Favorite nutrition book: *Prescription for Nutritional Healing* by James Balch, MD and Phyllis Balch, CNC
Favorite exercise: yoga
Favorite activity outside of work: traveling
What I do to treat myself: get a long massage
What I do to feel at peace: meditate
Wildest dream: to be a change agent on a global scale with unlimited funds to help people
Proudest moment: writing my first book, *40 Days to Power Living®*
Biggest challenge: keeping up with all of the inspirations that come to me
Health concerns I've cleared up: gastrointestinal symptoms of Crohn's disease
What I love about Integrative Nutrition: the network of people who want to transform lives
What I love about being a health counselor: changing lives
What I love about my star client, Victor: his new enthusiasm for life

ABOUT MY PRACTICE

Power Living Enterprises, Inc. | info@power-living.com | www.power-living.com

My counseling specialty is: life transformation. I help clients eat healthier, breathe deeper, work smarter, sleep more soundly, play more often and live more authentically.

My typical client is: a motivated individual who wants to change his or her life, not just diet. With my business background, I attract stressed-out executives and entrepreneurs, as well as anyone who wants to build a purposeful and powerful life. Given my integrative approach to managing Crohn's disease, I also attract people with digestive disorders, eating disorders, ADD and other anxiety and stress-related concerns.

What my clients love about my program: It's both practical and transformative. It meets them where they are and lasts a lifetime. My style is very empowering for clients. They learn how to be successful on their own terms, from the food they eat to the work they choose.

My favorite juicy question to ask my clients is: Who are you? Where are you? What must you do to be you? (These three core questions form the foundation of my Power Living® Practice.)

The top three results my clients get from working with me are: My clients achieve a greater understanding of their purpose and a desire for what I call Purpose With Results™. They also experience increased energy in the spiritual, mental, physical, emotional and environmental dimensions and develop a more conscious, positive and healthy way of eating and living.

In addition to one-on-one counseling, I also: write articles and books, produce Power Living® CDs and DVDs and run the Ta Yoga House in Harlem. I am a much sought-after motivational speaker, lecturing across the country to corporations and community groups, holding interactive workshops and leading teleclasses.

What I love about what I do: seeing the joy in clients' eyes when they finally articulate what is in their hearts and believe they can create an abundant life. I also get to meld skills from my years in the media, holistic health and yoga to help many people on a wider basis.

What is the message I'm getting out: I have an MBA from Harvard Business School, and I was one of the youngest vice presidents at MTV Networks, earning in the top 1% of the country. I pushed my body to the brink and almost died from a stress-induced ulcerated digestive system. I decided to leave my job to open one of the first yoga studios in Harlem, the Ta Yoga House. People thought I had lost my mind, but I was on a quest to create a more health-supportive lifestyle. At Integrative Nutrition I deepened my knowledge of cooking, digestion, stress management and food therapies. One day the brand Power Living® came to me. It is about combining healthy living with successful living. I help my clients figure out when to push hard and when to ease up, so they can live prosperous yet sustainable, healthy lives.

My greatest success so far: the scope of media exposure I've achieved by simply building relationships and telling my own story of transformation. I have been featured in TV, radio, print and online media around the world, from *O: The Oprah Magazine*, *Prevention Magazine* and *Yoga Journal* to CNN, NBC's *Today in New York* and a documentary on German TV. I am featured in Oprah's book, *Live Your Best Life!*. My current reach is to over 40 million people.

In the future, I see myself: creating an army of New World Purpose With Results Brokers™—people who are living from the heart, paving their own paths and making positive contributions to the universe.

CLIENT TESTIMONIAL

Victor

45 | owner of technology consulting firm | New York, NY

I love what I do, but before I worked with Teresa, I was doing it all the time. My personal life didn't exist. When I was not working, I would eat or sleep. I was prone to eating fast foods and quick order stuff because I wanted to be working, not spending time in the kitchen. I was getting up tired in the mornings and not enjoying myself. I went to Teresa for business coaching, but in short order she helped me to focus on other areas of my life that needed attention. Her coaching made me aware of how the pieces of my life—like food, career, health, education and fun—all fit together.

Before hiring Teresa I was always so tired that I could only do so much. Now I'm really looking forward to growing my business. I'm able to react faster to customer issues and help clients envision their future better. Every day I try to learn something new and do something I enjoy. I go out on the weekends, I've even started dating, I'm learning French and Spanish, and when I'm with my kids, I make sure I am doing something fun with them. I hadn't taken a vacation in years, and now I go somewhere every couple of months.

Teresa was able to get me moving. I appreciated that she was so firm with me and got me to commit to doing things. It made all the difference to have someone inspiring me and motivating me.

Alex Jamieson

Class of 2003 | New York, NY and Los Angeles, CA

Life is a feast, and most poor suckers are starving to death!

—Patrick Dennis, Auntie Mame

Job before Integrative Nutrition: health-supportive personal chef
Childhood ambition: to be President of the United States
Favorite snack food: air-popped popcorn with olive oil, sea salt and kinako soy flour
Favorite healthy food: kale sautéed with garlic and olive oil
Favorite nutrition book: my own! *The Great American Detox Book* by Alex Jamieson
Favorite exercise: snowboarding or yoga
Favorite activity outside of work: watching movies with my husband
What I do to treat myself: get massages and facials
What I do to feel at peace: meditate
Wildest dream: to be able to fly or to speak every language on the planet
Proudest moment: publishing my first book
Biggest challenge: balancing travel with staying healthy
Health concerns I've cleared up: low energy, sugar addiction, migraine headaches, weight gain and candida
What I love about Integrative Nutrition: the long-term support and the amazing people I met there
What I love about being a health counselor: I learn so much from my clients about health, food—and about myself! It's a non-stop education.
What I love about my star client, Lucy: She is willing to try anything and has a great sense of humor!

ABOUT MY PRACTICE

Healthy Chef Alex | alex@healthychefalex.com | www.healthychefalex.com

My counseling specialty is: helping women between the ages of 23 and 55 increase their energy, lose weight, reduce their health concerns and get rid of their sugar and caffeine dependencies.

My typical client is: "sick and tired of being sick and tired" and wants to get in touch with what her body really needs. She wants to detox from an unhealthy lifestyle, or she wants support in transitioning to a vegetarian or vegan diet.

The top three results my clients get from working with me are: increased energy, better sleep and weight loss. They learn to enjoy simple, whole foods like fruits and vegetables, and their tastes change quickly and dramatically. They get their spark back, they lose weight and their thinking clears up. They take their lives in new, exciting directions.

What my clients love about my program: We go into all areas of their lives to uncover the real reasons behind their health concerns. My clients appreciate that we have a good time and try new and fun ideas. They love how nonjudgmental and supportive I am.

My favorite juicy question to ask my clients is: How does your love life affect your health and your food cravings?

What I love about what I do: I can help people in a meaningful way to improve their health for the long term. I love hearing an "aha!" from a client when they begin to understand their body better. I love sharing in my clients' personal victories.

In addition to one-on-one counseling, I also: speak at high schools, colleges and national health groups. I take people on health food store tours, offer cooking classes and write articles on food and healing for national publications.

How I get my message out to a wider audience: My husband, Morgan Spurlock, created *Super Size Me*, the hit documentary about American fast food. My detox diet restored his health, so when the movie came out I was thrust into the spotlight as a chef and a health expert. My book was published by Rodale Press, and I began traveling around the country speaking to universities, health conferences and advocacy groups. I've spoken to national media outlets in over 20 countries. I've been on CNN, Jimmy Kimmel, and many talk shows and radio broadcasts. The confidence and training that I received at Integrative Nutrition prepared me for the challenges of national interviews and public speaking.

My greatest success so far: speaking at the national American Heart Association conference— they loved my talk!

In the future, I see myself: writing at least three more books, becoming a homeopath and helping to change the way our culture views healthcare. I envision our world transitioning to a preventative care structure, and every child learning how to grow and cook their own food.

CLIENT TESTIMONIAL

Lucy

52 | educator | Jarrettsville, MD

I'd been a vegetarian for 25 years but never learned how to do it in a healthy way. I was eating a lot of prepackaged, high-sodium vegetarian foods like fake chicken nuggets, plus I was a big fan of butter and cheeses. I had hot flashes, headaches, weight gain and not a lot of energy. I was diagnosed with a dead thyroid and went on medication. While investigating weight loss options, I came across Alex's website and saw her connection to *Super Size Me*. I saw the movie and knew I wanted to learn from her.

Alex taught me that there is such a big world of wholesome, good food out there. I bought all the whole grains she has told me about—they are like little cells of energy! I discovered how to eat with the seasons, for instance, lettuce and light foods in the summer and squashes, potatoes and heartier foods in the winter months. I've been able to tune into my body and feed it what it wants, like squashes, greens and pickles.

Now I have loads more energy. I don't eat out of emotion or boredom. I sleep a lot better. I feel better about myself, and in turn, I feel better about everybody around me. In the mornings I go to the gym, and I'm not immediately exhausted after work. I enjoy gardening, biking and yoga—it's great to have the energy. I'm really learning who I am and what my body needs. I'm looking forward to getting off my thyroid medication, staying healthy, living longer and teaching my grandkids how to fuel their bodies properly. If they start now, what a journey in life they could have! I thank my lucky stars for Alex!

Andrea Beaman

Class of 1999 | New York, NY

Whether you think you CAN or think you CAN't, you're right.

—Henry Ford

Job before Integrative Nutrition: executive assistant at MTV Networks
Childhood ambition: to be a veterinarian
Favorite snack food: homemade organic popcorn, popped in peanut oil, sprinkled with sea salt and drizzled with organic butter
Favorite healthy food: roasted fish with fresh herbs and olive oil, with a side of sautéed vegetables, and a baby mesclun green salad with honey mustard vinaigrette
Favorite kitchen tool: my Japanese-style knife with a 7-inch blade
Favorite exercise: hatha yoga, walking or jogging
Favorite activity outside of work: eating out with friends and family at organic restaurants
What I do to treat myself: eat the best food as often as possible and surround myself with people I love
What I do to feel at peace: stay in my "center," honor myself, meditate and breathe
Wildest dream: to have a popular national TV show that inspires millions of human beings to get healthy and enjoy life to the fullest
Proudest moment: hearing my doctor tell me that I've healed my abnormal thyroid and heart murmur and that I am normal and healthy
Biggest challenge: learning to fully trust my intuition and follow my gut instincts
Health concerns I've cleared up: thyroid disease, weak immune system and heart murmur
What I love about Integrative Nutrition: the warm environment and amazing community. It's a school that makes you stop and think.
What I love about my star client, Lisa: her courage to try something new

ABOUT MY PRACTICE

Andrea Beaman, HHC | Andrea@AndreaBeaman.com | www.AndreaBeaman.com

My counseling specialty is: teaching people how to get the best quality food into their lives in the easiest possible ways. This includes both physical and emotional food.

My typical clients are: questioning their health, lifestyle and eating habits, unhappy with their current weight, and possibly sick with a disease. They are seeking to make improvements to enhance their overall quality of life. Self-motivated people are attracted to working with me. They're done with medication and the medical establishment, and they don't want to be a statistic.

What my clients love about my program: the flexibility and freedom. I don't have a "do-it-or-die" philosophy. I teach them to do the best they can as often as they can, love themselves in the process and just keep moving forward. I try to shift their focus to the positive as much as possible. As clients get into the habit of focusing on good things, those positive things they do for themselves will grow.

The top three results my clients get from working with me are: greater knowledge of food and how it can affect their health and life, increased energy and weight loss. A lot of changes start to happen for people when they get even a little bit healthier. They feel better physically, and then they want to change their jobs or improve their relationships. It's exciting to watch.

My favorite juicy question to ask my clients: What positive choices have you made for yourself since I saw you last?

In addition to one-on-one counseling, I also: teach natural foods cooking classes and write books. I often appear in the print media or on TV as a nationally recognized food expert and inspirational speaker.

The message I want to get out: We don't have to be sick, diseased and doped up on medications that aren't really curing our ailments. Prescription drugs do not get to the root cause of disease, yet millions of people are hooked. As a society, we are losing touch with ourselves, which is a dangerous situation. My inspiration to speak out comes from my heart. I love people, and I want my fellow human beings to experience all the joys of a balanced, healthy life. The healthier we are in mind and body, the better this earth will be for all people.

What I love about what I do: guiding people to take full responsibility for their lives and their health. Teaching people how to obtain the freedom to be in their natural state—vibrantly healthy and loving life—is a great job!

My greatest success so far: self-publishing my books on health, healing and food (*The Whole Truth* and *The Whole Truth Eating and Recipe Guide*). I have a third book on the way, and many more to come in the future. I was also featured on Bravo TV's *Top Chef*, and on the popular morning show *The View*.

In the future, I see myself: doing what I'm doing now, only on a bigger scale, reaching more people. I will be hosting a highly successful healthy lifestyle and cooking television show that makes taking care of yourself fun, enjoyable and easy as organic pie!

CLIENT TESTIMONIAL

Lisa

38 | director of product licensing | New York, NY

I work in the hectic, crazy fashion industry. I'm passionate about my main hobby, yoga, and I'm married with a new baby. With my history of an eating disorder, my diet has never been good. I would snack all day on power bars, low-fat cookies, low-fat chips, various forms of sugar and, of course, coffee. I was in my late 30s and always very tired and often sick. I was trying to get pregnant and very concerned that unless I ate better, I would not be able to conceive.

When I met Andrea, she "beamed" with health and seemed incredibly intuitive and compassionate. Before working with her, I never cooked anything, but I really enjoyed cooking with her one-on-one and in cooking classes. Now I eat much more than I used to and have not gained any unnecessary weight. For breakfast I'll have oatmeal or eggs and cheese, for lunch a huge salad with seasonal veggies or an egg salad sandwich, and dinner varies but I try to eat a balanced meal. I walk and run more and try to spend some time outside in the park. I also cook more and experiment with new foods.

I'm grateful to Andrea for opening my eyes to how much my life, psyche and health are affected by what I eat. I got pregnant in just five months, which I attribute to my body getting healthy enough to conceive. I have much more energy, my bowel movements are better, and my skin tone is healthier (before, it was green/grayish). I plan to continue to eat a healthy diet and pass that habit on to my husband and children. I'm looking forward to cooking more with my family, and to our leading healthy, disease-free lives.

4

Changing Careers

It is said that the average American will change careers at least five times during the course of his or her working life. There are those who bemoan this fact, citing the lack of security that comes with the abandonment of one career path, or mourning the loss of individuals' trust in corporations. We at Integrative Nutrition take a different stance. Change brings fresh energy to our lives. Having the opportunity to shift careers is an absolute freedom. Gone are the days when people were trapped by one right way to earn a living. There is no longer a need to shrug your shoulders at boredom or frustration in a job, brushing these off as part of making your way. If you wake up every morning dreading your workday, or even if you like what you do but long for more meaning in your occupation, you can change.

Not only can you change, we say you should. Being gratified in your career is a crucial piece of maintaining health. In fact, we view it as so important that we list it as one of the four main ingredients in a concept we call primary food. Along with healthy relationships, regular physical activity and spiritual practice, a career that excites and fulfills you is an essential component of a happy, healthy life.

Many students come to Integrative Nutrition to start a new career. They are lawyers, financial planners, photographers, technology consultants, teachers or others who desire work that is rewarding and makes a positive difference in the world. We support all of these students in their brave transitions. The stories in this chapter demonstrate the joy that our students gain in becoming professional health counselors, in adopting a new career that is in alignment with their hopes, dreams and values. As you read them, delight in the power we all have to change and to create work that nourishes our very core.

Monica Shah

Class of 2005 | New York, NY

If a person is living out his Personal Legend, he knows everything he needs to know. There is only one thing that makes a dream impossible to achieve: the fear of failure.

—Paulo Coelho

Job before Integrative Nutrition: brand manager at a large beauty company
Childhood ambition: to be a veterinarian
Favorite snack food: Fage Greek yogurt with agave nectar, vanilla extract and strawberries
Favorite healthy food: raw kale salad with lemon juice, olive oil, golden raisins and pine nuts
Favorite nutrition book: *Eat, Drink, and Be Healthy* by Walter Willett, MD
Favorite exercise: hiking
Favorite activity outside of work: long dinners with friends
Favorite vacation spot: Maui, Hawaii
Craziest thing I've ever done: jumped off a mountain in a hang glider
Wildest dream: to travel around the world and learn new languages in each country
Proudest moment: the day I got into the Kellogg School of Management
Biggest challenge: staying organized and focused on the details. I'm a "big picture" person.
Health concerns I've cleared up: sugar cravings, extra weight, low energy and food sensitivities
What I love about Integrative Nutrition: The school gave me the opportunity to leave a career that didn't fit to pursue one that I love.
What I love about being a health counselor: helping people see that they are supremely intelligent and know best how to take care of themselves
What I love about my star client, Laurel: She tries all the suggestions and is committed to improving her health.

ABOUT MY PRACTICE

Ideal Balance | Monica@idealbalanceinc.com | www.idealbalanceinc.com

My counseling specialty is: working with busy professionals who want to find more balance in their lives through nutrition, exercise and self-care. Clients like working with me because I share their corporate background. They see my commitment to them and know that I left a very high paying job to do this work because I believe in it.

My typical client is: a professional woman in her 20s or 30s who suffers from low energy, stress, excess weight, mood swings and/or digestive issues. She wants to increase her energy, focus through the whole day, lose weight and feel fantastic.

What my clients love about my program: My suggestions are simple and work well into a busy schedule. I love to keep things interesting, sending my clients new ideas and suggestions. I give my clients the space to hear themselves and follow their own innate wisdom, while giving them small suggestions to propel them to radiant health.

My favorite juicy question to ask my clients is: If you were to wave a magic wand and make all the changes in your life that you want, what would your life look like?

The top three results my clients get from working with me are: balanced, consistent energy throughout the day; weight loss; and increased levels of professional and personal success. Plus they quit smoking, quit sugar and reduce their caffeine. Almost all my clients learn to exercise regularly. I am a former triathlete, and clients really like that I show them how to fit exercise into their lives.

In addition to one-on-one counseling, I also: conduct group programs, workshops and classes.

Why I changed careers: I had just graduated from business school, was working 80 hours a week in the corporate world, and was really unhappy at my job. I was stressed out and completely addicted to sugar. At the same time, I was passionate about nutrition and would study it on the side. I realized how out of alignment my life was and that I wanted to do work that was meaningful to me. Integrative Nutrition gave me an official structure for pursuing my passion as a career. My sugar cravings cleared up, my mood lifted and I began to understand that I have the power to create a life that makes me happy.

What I love about what I do: the creativity of this work and how I can create something new with it anytime. Integrative Nutrition gave me a career that allows me to live in integrity. I ask my clients to make healthy choices and pay attention to their bodies, and it comes from a strong place because I do the same every day.

My greatest success so far: leaving the stability and financial security of my corporate job to follow my passion, and building a successful private practice in just nine months.

In the future, I see myself: creating more communities and discussion groups with past and current clients. I want clients to connect with one another to share their infinite wisdom through classes, retreats, phone calls and events. There is power and transformation in creating a community.

CLIENT TESTIMONIAL

Laurel

27 | actress | New York, NY

I'm a Midwestern girl who moved to New York to pursue my passion for acting. I had a wonderful traditional upbringing in Cleveland, and family is very important to me. So when my mom's two older sisters died from cancer it threw me for a loop. I took a step back from acting, was dealing with a break-up, and felt overweight, apathetic and weighed down. I wanted to rebuild and take control of my life in a positive way.

I met Monica at yoga class. Her program sounded fantastic. Instead of weight loss, we made overall health my goal. Monica introduced me to nutrient-rich, fiber-rich foods and taught me to cook for myself. I'm sleeping better and I feel more confident and relaxed. I've worked my body into the best physical shape I've had in 10 years. I have many auditions each week, and I've hired a manager. I think this is because I've said yes to taking care of myself and to going after what I want.

I'm a perfectionist and a Type A personality, so I love that Monica breaks everything down into clear and simple steps. She makes it easy to be healthy. Monica truly empowered me to be who I am without apology, to acknowledge and accept myself. I'm confident in my future and more excited than ever to watch it unfold.

Rose Payne

Class of 2001 | Marlton, NJ

What would you do if you knew you could not fail?

—Albert Schweitzer

Job before Integrative Nutrition: hairstylist
Childhood ambition: to be a hairstylist
Favorite snack food: almonds covered in honey and sesame seeds
Favorite healthy food: butternut squash and aduki bean soup
Favorite nutrition book: *Radical Healing* by Rudolph Ballantine, MD
Favorite type of exercise: couples dancing
Favorite activity outside of work: sleep
What I do to treat myself: buy expensive clothes
What I do to feel at peace: walk outside
Wildest dream: living vibrantly past the age of 100
Proudest moment: speaking at Integrative Nutrition's 2005 graduation
Biggest challenge: public speaking
Health concerns I've cleared up: cysts and headaches
What I love about Integrative Nutrition: the brilliant curriculum and the community
What I love about being a health counselor: flexible hours, great clients and
making a difference
What I love about my star client, Phyllis: her beautiful pioneering spirit,
never-say-die attitude and unrelenting love for her partner and her friends

ABOUT MY PRACTICE

High Level Wellness, LLC | highlevelwellness@earthlink.net | highlevelwellnessonline.com

My counseling specialties are: sugar addiction, women's health issues, puzzling conditions and individual eating plans.

My typical client is: a woman who is confused about her relationship with food, frustrated by her bodily health and ready to make transformational changes.

The top three results my clients get from working with me are: resolving their particular health concerns, having a new friendly relationship with food and increasing their energy. Almost everyone I work with has very good digestion when we're done. Their busy lives become more manageable. I also see them become much happier in their relationships.

My favorite juicy question to ask my clients is: Can you tell me your life story?

What my clients love about my program: It is fun, educational and effective all at the same time. I always set my clients up for success. My method includes a specific manner of listening that allows me to mirror back what the client already knows about their body and overall condition. I can shortcut them to manageable changes that they can make right away. We don't waste any time, and they get results very quickly.

In addition to one-on-one counseling, I also: do educational training seminars, corporate workshops and other public speaking engagements.

Why I changed careers: I had a 20-year career as a hairdresser and loved every minute. My life in general was good: I had a strong spiritual practice, was eating well and exercising regularly, and had a wonderful relationship and family. Then one day I looked around my salon and realized there were no old hairdressers, and I wasn't getting any younger. What was I going to do with the rest of my life? As soon as I began my search, I met someone who had attended Integrative Nutrition. I enrolled and started my new career as a holistic health counselor.

What I love about what I do: Each day is totally different than the day before. It never gets boring. Plus, I am truly blessed to have a community of health counselors working in my practice with me. We have wonderful jobs, assisting others in their transformations. It doesn't get any better than this!

My greatest success so far: speaking in front of 1,200 people. My latest "just for fun" success has been moving the practice to a new location—our own wellness center. We are providing our individual and group nutrition counseling, and adding new educational workshops and guest speakers. The new center is on a beautiful two-acre piece of property with a garden, labyrinth, creek and raspberry patch.

In the future, I see: unlimited possibilities. I am an advocate for health counseling as an industry. Everybody should be given an opportunity to heal through this modality. Hence, I will do everything I can, whether it is coaching, teaching or hand-holding, to support and develop successful health counselors.

CLIENT TESTIMONIAL

Phyllis

59 | private detective | Woodbury, NJ

I was told I wouldn't live to see my 21st birthday. By the age of 25 I had survived nearly a dozen surgeries. Fortunately, I recovered and I was able to have a career in law enforcement. I eventually started my private detective agency, which I absolutely love.

Prior to working with Rose I had suffered with gastro-esophageal reflux and adult asthma for many years. I was taking numerous medications, including using three different inhalers. Eventually my reflux became acute. The doctor suggested surgery might be my only option. That's when I made an appointment with Rose.

With each session I made small upgrades to my diet that resulted in huge gains to my health, energy and general outlook. I felt no suffering or sacrifice as I ate more salads, fruits and vegetables and less dairy, meats and processed foods. As my condition improved I became aware of a level of zest I had never experienced before. I had been ill for most of my life and assumed there was nothing I could do about it. But after six months of working with Rose I have never looked or felt healthier. I no longer use any medication for asthma or reflux. I lost 20 pounds and feel much better. So this is what being healthy feels like!

Rose is a unique person and a natural at counseling. She's easy to talk to, and she hears me in a way that allows her to actually answer my questions. She had great strategies to ensure my success, and I never felt like I was following a formula. There was no such thing as failure. I now look forward to a future with far fewer pills and doctors. I still wonder how I can adequately thank Rose for a gift this great.

Brenda Horton

Class of 2004 | New York, NY

God bless the child that has his own. —Billie Holiday

Job before Integrative Nutrition: accountant
Childhood ambition: to be a doctor
Favorite snack food: dried mango and pineapple slices
Favorite healthy food: green medley (a combo of kale, collard and mustard greens, sautéed with shitake mushrooms and onions in olive oil)
Favorite nutrition book: *Back to Eden* by Jethro Kloss
Favorite exercise: spinning or aerobics
Favorite activity outside of work: scuba diving
What I do to treat myself: travel to exotic places
What I do to feel at peace: meditate each and every day
Wildest dream: learn how to fly a plane and fly to Costa Rica
Proudest moment: opening my wellness studio, La Pura Vida, one month before my graduation from Integrative Nutrition, with 10 paying clients to start
Biggest challenge: getting my family on the right track food-wise, since we have a history of high blood pressure, diabetes and obesity
Health concerns that I've cleared up: severe eczema and adult acne
What I love about Integrative Nutrition: They gave me the confidence to stand up for what I truly believed in and to be myself.
What I love about being a health counselor: I help people turn their lives around.
What I love about my star client, Kira: She was willing to work together with me on changing her life, and she believed it was all possible.

ABOUT MY PRACTICE

La Pura Vida | thepurelife-lpv@nyc.rr.com

My counseling specialties are: weight loss, diabetes, high blood pressure and cholesterol, and lack of self-esteem.

My typical client is: usually in a state of desperation, not knowing where to turn after having been everywhere else with no results. He or she wants to lose weight, control cravings, incorporate exercise into their lives and control or minimize health issues. Many are women facing an enormous amount of stress at home and at work, and they've developed eating habits that stress out their bodies more, like eating on the run, eating convenience foods and not drinking enough water.

What my clients love about my program: the sense that someone truly cares about them and what's happening in their lives, the flexibility of my program and my massage.

My favorite juicy question to ask my clients is: Who are you and how do you feel about yourself?

The top three results my clients get from working with me are: weight loss, a newfound sense of self-esteem and the ability to believe in themselves and what they can accomplish in their lives. They each completely change their eating habits, calm down, learn to value themselves and move out of unhealthy relationships or stressful situations. The tension that was in their faces is gone and their skin looks beautiful. I love to see that the changes they've made are so long-lasting.

In addition to one-on-one counseling, I also: offer Thai massage and reflexology sessions, group and one-on-one meditations, fasting and chakra cleansings. Integrative Nutrition encouraged me to personalize my program and do what I was excited about, so after graduation I flew to Thailand and learned Thai massage. Now I have a wellness business that helps my clients take care of the total self, inside and out.

Why I changed careers: I was an accountant for 20 years, but I always knew that wasn't who I really was. I was into exercise, doing personal training on the side and studying herbal medicine. Then I found Integrative Nutrition. Since then my life has changed so much, I have to keep pinching myself! If not for the school, I would still be an accountant, sitting in front of my calculator, dreaming about this life. Instead, I've taken my dreams and put them into action!

What I love about what I do: The flexibility—I love the fact that I make my own hours. I love to help people, and I am always able to learn something new from my clients.

My greatest success so far: being appointed Health and Wellness editor for *Jolie*, a nationally syndicated magazine. I will be helping readers learn about avoiding diabetes, improving digestion, increasing their lifespan and finding their right diet. I really want people to understand that creating health is about the whole you, and that it is worth your time and attention. Working for *Jolie* is an exciting, unlimited opportunity for me to get this message out.

In the future, I see myself: incorporating acupuncture, Oriental, Western and herbal medicines into my practice.

CLIENT TESTIMONIAL

Kira

35 | accountant | Brooklyn, NY

As a person in finance, my life can be sedentary, so I do a lot of things outside the office, like go out with friends and volunteer. For example, I've been a mentor with Big Brothers, Big Sisters for nine years. At the time I met Brenda, I needed to lose weight and had signs of arthritis in my knees. I was nurturing and helping a lot of other people, but I needed help to take better care of myself.

We made my diet changes slowly and found out how my emotions were tied to what I would eat. I learned to eat for the purpose of nutrition, to slow down and to find healthy substitutes. In six months I dropped 19 pounds and many inches. Now I can shop in regular dress stores, jog for 30 minutes on a treadmill and climb the subway stairs without getting winded.

Improving my nutrition helped me gain confidence in other areas. I changed to a less stressful work environment where I am happier in my job. I actually take downtime to read, meditate, write in my journal or take a walk by myself. I also make time to pamper myself and to go to the gym. The biggest gift Brenda gave me was helping me get back to myself. She taught me that in order to help others, I have to help me, too. I'm really grateful for that.

5

Holistic and Successful

Make no mistake: holistic health has gone mainstream. Organic food, yoga, chiropractic care and massage therapy are no longer reserved for a select few. They are common practices, and people around the globe are using them to improve their health. This trend is bound to continue. After all, healthier bodies create healthier minds, and healthier minds inevitably lead to greater happiness. With such certain and positive results, the holistic health field cannot help but flourish. We at Integrative Nutrition are not alone in our belief that the field has an unlimited potential for growth.

This potential creates the opportunity for our graduates to thrive in their work. It is possible for them to do what they love and get paid well for it. Beyond the stellar training we provide around nutrition and counseling, we also offer in-depth business education. We recognize that in order to become powerful agents of change, students need to understand how to run and market their businesses, and they need to be richly rewarded for their work. Their own profound success will fuel them to carry on, and make them shining examples to their clients of how abundant the universe can be.

The graduates featured in this chapter were already experts in their fields when they came to our school. Integrative Nutrition bolstered their careers. They are living proof of the might of the holistic health approach, of how it can transform the lives of clients and support its practitioners to live in ways they have always imagined.

Angel A. Orozco

Class of 2003 | Miami Beach, FL

Who looks outside, dreams;
who looks inside, awakes.

—Sherry Rogers, MD

Job: massage therapist and health counselor
Childhood ambition: to be financially independent
Favorite snack food: fresh fruits with mixed nuts
Favorite healthy food: watercress salad with grilled seitan
Favorite nutrition book: *Detoxify or Die* by Sherry Rogers, MD
Favorite exercise: spinning, weight training or skiing
Favorite activity outside of work: watching a good film
What I do to treat myself: get a spa treatment
What I do to feel at peace: take a deep breath and smile
Wildest dream: to live in a world where everyone is at peace, where kids are not bombarded with unhealthy advertising and where it is easy to live in a healthy environment
Proudest moment: giving a 78-year-old client a new treatment that allowed him to move without restriction in his shoulder, which had been frozen for over 20 years
Biggest challenge: educating in health a population that is so confused about what is good for them
Health concerns that I've cleared up: acid reflux, asthma, ulcers and skin allergies
What I love about Integrative Nutrition: learning that nutrition goes beyond what we eat and that everybody has to figure out individually what works for them
What I love about being a health counselor: helping people in pain become happy and pain-free
What I love about my star client, Karen: seeing all the positive changes in her life

ABOUT MY PRACTICE

BodySense, Inc. | angel@bodysenseusa.com | www.bodysenseusa.com

My counseling specialties are: life coaching and nutrition education. BodySense is a full-service spa where I also specialize in pain management, beauty and relaxation.

My typical client is: a woman who wants to live a healthier, pain-free life. I see many well-off spa clientele and also people with pain issues from disease, TMJ or auto accidents. Integrative Nutrition gave me a strong background in nutrition, so discussing food is part of my daily interaction with all my clients.

What my clients love about my program: I'm very passionate about what I do. Everything I teach comes from the heart. Clients like that I'm outspoken and affectionate. My program is also very complete. What I promote is healthy living. Health comes from more than what you eat. It's from good exercise, a positive relationship with your spouse or parents and being connected spiritually. People aren't used to thinking about health in these ways.

My favorite juicy question to ask my clients: Do you eat dairy or consume aspartame?

The top three results my clients get from working with me are: feeling better, finding a healthier body weight and getting motivated. For a lot of people, pain they have had their whole lives goes away.

In addition to one-on-one counseling, I also: give massage therapy and electro-acupuncture, and teach lectures, do health store tours and teach spinning classes.

Why I incorporated nutrition into my business: When I studied pain management, I started seeing the relationship of nutrition to pain and health. When people take certain foods out of their diet, like wheat or dairy, it changes their pain. I had one client with fibromyalgia go off of aspartame and reduce his pain by 50%. I saw kids clear up their asthma when they stopped drinking milk. I found it fascinating. I became hungry for more knowledge to help my clients. When I learned about Integrative Nutrition, I knew it was exactly what I needed.

What I love about what I do: I actually get money for giving massage and educating people—things I love to do. It used to be that I'd be at a party and suddenly people would ask me to talk about health. Now I give workshops—it's the same thing, only I get paid! I also love that I've had the opportunity to bring this work to Miami, when it hasn't been that well known down here.

My greatest success so far: In the last few years BodySense has grown from a small massage therapy office to a holistic wellness center with over 20 different practitioners. We've opened a second center, with yoga, tai chi, meditation, a juice bar and special lectures. Word about us is spreading. I've had the chance to work with many celebrities including Ricky Martin, Elton John, Donatella Versace, Jean-Claude Van Damme and Sandra Bernhard.

In the future, I see: BodySense Wellness Centers all over the US and abroad.

CLIENT TESTIMONIAL

Karen

34 | massage therapist and spinning instructor | Miami, FL

I used to work in real estate but I didn't like it at all. It was too stressful for me, so I became a massage therapist. I love giving massage. It's great that just by using my hands and setting a good intention for someone I can help them so much. When I'm not working I love to teach spinning classes. I get a great workout while helping other people reduce their stress. It gives me a lot of satisfaction.

I met Angel when I was starting out to be a massage therapist. I wanted to be involved in a massage therapy environment, and I ended up at his center. At that time I used to drink alcohol and eat a lot of meat, chicken and fatty foods. Those foods would keep me up at night, and I couldn't digest them well. For almost a year I had been trying to lose 10 pounds. I was going to the gym and trying different diets, but I couldn't lose the weight. Angel taught me that I was treating my body in ways that weren't good for me.

I changed to a healthy vegetarian diet, and I feel so much better. I lost the 10 pounds without really trying. My digestion is good, and I don't have sleep problems anymore. People around me tell me that I look so thin, so healthy. When they comment, it gives me an opportunity to talk to them about healthy eating. Because I've changed my diet, my attitude and energy has changed 100%. Angel is a great teacher and mentor. He's my inspiration, and I am really grateful I've found him. Right now I'm completely happy in my life. I've found everything that I've been looking for.

Danielle O'Connell

Class of 2004 | New York, NY

There are only two ways to live your life. One is as though nothing is a miracle. The other is as though everything is a miracle. -Albert Einstein

Job: Pilates and yoga instructor and health counselor
Childhood ambition: to have my own business
Favorite snack food: dark-chocolate–covered raisins
Favorite healthy food: steamed kale and quinoa with lemon juice and garlic chili flax oil
Favorite kitchen tool: my blender
Favorite exercise: playing with my two-year-old
Favorite activity outside of work: rock climbing
What I do to treat myself: take a nap
Craziest thing I've ever done: jumped out of a plane
Wildest dream: taking a safari in Africa
Proudest moment: giving birth to my daughter
Biggest challenge: how to get more sleep
Health concerns I've cleared up: sugar addiction, candida and sinus problems
What I love about Integrative Nutrition: how they acknowledge that "primary food"—career, spiritual practice, exercise and relationships—is just as important to our health as the food we eat
What I love about being a health counselor: I get to teach what I am passionate about.
What I love about my star client, Lizo: She is open-minded and trusting.

ABOUT MY PRACTICE

UrbanWellness | danielle@urbanwellness.com | www.urbanwellness.com

My counseling specialty is: addressing sugar cravings and candida. I've been a personal trainer for over 10 years, but for the last five years I've specialized in Pilates and yoga exclusively.

My typical client is: motivated and wants to feel great, not just look great (although that happens too!). I work with people who need to find what works best for their body and lifestyle in terms of food, exercise and self-care.

What my clients love about my program: My combination of nutrition and exercise accelerates their progress. They learn so much about themselves. All of a sudden they become aware of how food affects them and how great moving, breathing and using their muscles can make them feel, both mentally and physically.

My favorite juicy question to ask my clients is: What are your goals?

The top three results my clients get from working with me are: taking charge of their lives and eating, reducing cravings and losing excess weight. I teach my clients the relationship between their health, mood, eating habits and any other issues in their lives. Usually once they make that connection, all their other healing falls into place.

In addition to one-on-one counseling, I also: am a Pilates and yoga teacher.

Why I combine nutrition, yoga and Pilates: For people who are really ready for amazing changes in their lives, this combination allows them to make a lot of progress in a short period of time, as the energy in their bodies shifts very quickly. Both Pilates and yoga strengthen and stretch the body, improve circulation and breathing, and reduce pain. They change the way people carry themselves and improve their general sense of well-being. They also improve the ability to genuinely focus and clear the mind, as does cutting out junk foods. My Pilates and health counseling clients become much more clear-headed and generally make healthier choices for themselves.

What I love about what I do: I have great clients and a flexible schedule. It's especially rewarding when I'm able to help my clients think outside of the box to find something that really works for them as a unique individual. I'm always amazed at how clients take that knowledge forward on their own and make positive changes.

My greatest success so far: taking the leap of faith to actually work on my own, and creating my Pilates for Pregnancy DVD.

In the future, I see myself: enjoying the flexibility of my business and spending more time with my family.

CLIENT TESTIMONIAL

Lizo

34 | actress and singer | San Francisco, CA

I used to be a Wall Street girl, but when I moved west from New York City, I got into acting and singing. I really love it. My work with Danielle deepened my acting ability, though my program with her started out about weight loss and other health problems. I had terrible PMS with mood swings and trouble with my digestive system. Someone recommended that I talk to Danielle. She seemed to have a glow from the inside and said it was because of her work at Integrative Nutrition. I definitely wanted to work with her.

I created a better connection to my body and started to notice what it craves. I noticed that my body did not react well to dairy and that it was not asking for chocolate but kale! Then things just sort of started to clear up. The mood swings went away, my digestion problems turned around, and my skin began to clear up. I feel more peaceful, grounded and in touch with the world around me. In my acting I find that I have a better connection to my emotions.

Danielle is an exceptional listener. She opened my eyes to the concept that nourishing myself is about how I take care of myself in all parts of my life, not just food. I now have a lifelong interest in health and my body. I'm looking forward to getting stronger at nurturing myself and giving my body what it needs as I grow older.

Deborah Dunn

Class of 2003 | Montclair, NJ

Stay in the center of the circle and let all things take their course.

—Lao Tzu

Job: yoga studio owner, yoga instructor and health counselor
Childhood ambition: I had no idea of direction or possibilities.
Favorite snack food: dates, raw almonds and raw cashews
Favorite healthy food: big salad with kale, arugula, avocado, cherry tomatoes, red pepper, kalamata olives, raw broccoli, grated carrots and shredded red cabbage with carrot-ginger dressing
Favorite kitchen tool: my Vita Mix blender
Favorite activity outside of work: spending time with friends and a cup of tea
Favorite vacation spot: India
Craziest thing I've ever done: volunteered to have knives thrown at me in a Mexican circus act
Wildest dream: being an honored teacher
Proudest moment: leading the first women's AA meeting in Pune, India
Biggest challenge: gracefully balancing managing my business and parenting my three teenage daughters
Health concerns I've cleared up: I just navigated through menopause with grace and ease. I am the first woman on both sides of my family to do this without a hysterectomy for a few generations.
What I love about Integrative Nutrition: the totally empowering, unique, nonconformist teaching and the lifelong community of like-minded people
What I love about being a health counselor: doing amazing work that I totally believe in to guide people to live incredible, healthy and balanced lives
What I love about my star client, Rajan: his total commitment to his health and wellness

ABOUT MY PRACTICE

Balanced Wellness | Ddebdun@aol.com

My counseling specialty is: working with people in recovery, with women with mid-life issues and with kids.

My typical client is: in recovery and wants to address other health issues in their life, such as food cravings. My own experiences of addiction, recovery and healing make me a great counselor to others in recovery.

What my clients love about my program: They're able to achieve their goals, while feeling loved, supported and guided in the process. I make them feel special.

My favorite juicy question to ask my clients is: If you were to have exactly what you want in the bedroom, what would that be?

The top three results my clients get from working with me are: weight loss, reduced cravings and getting off prescription drugs.

In addition to one-on-one counseling, I also: teach yoga, meditation, breath work, cooking classes and raw food prep classes, and prepare healing foods for private clients.

Why I incorporated health counseling into my business: I was a yoga instructor interested in health and wellness, but I had no idea how to turn my knowledge and experience into a successful business. Integrative Nutrition was my "holistic business school." Now I own a yoga studio where I see my health counseling clients and teach yoga, cooking classes and spirituality workshops. It is a profitable business that I am absolutely connected to. My counseling program includes nutrition, one yoga class per week, Reiki and pranayama breathing. The combination is very powerful for my clients.

What I love about what I do: working with people to make simple and major changes in their lives.

My greatest success so far: working with my client Rajan, from India, who was diagnosed with leukemia. By making changes in his diet, he greatly improved his blood tests. He has much more energy and he has hope.

In the future, I see myself: working with many people here and in other parts of the world, helping them come to a place of balance and wellness through simple, whole nourishment.

CLIENT TESTIMONIAL

Rajan

50 | human resources consultant | Pune, India

In 2003 I was diagnosed with chronic leukemia. My doctors gave me the best, most advanced drug to manage the disease, but my body could not tolerate it. The drug impaired my liver function and I became jaundiced. They had to stop my medication. I wasn't sure what to do next. Around this time Deborah entered my life.

Deborah saw that my diet was too heavy for my liver to handle. I was a nonvegetarian, eating red meat and fish. I loved pastry for breakfast and took a lot of milk, like yogurt drinks and milk in my tea. My typical Indian diet also included wheat chapatis, steamed rice, eggs, and vegetables cooked in oil. We changed my food to include salad, leafy greens, steamed summer vegetables, fresh fruit and plenty of water. I kept a journal about what I ate and how I felt. I walked, booked massages and took a 10-day retreat to rest my body.

Making these changes was easy—it felt like no work at all. Deborah is an excellent motivator and a very fine human being. She never talked from a pedestal. She shared her own experience and related to my concerns. We worked together here during her time in India, and then by e-mail after she returned home. Within one month of making changes, my liver recovered and I was able to go back on the medication. Now I am tolerating the drug very well, and my liver function is perfect!

6

Bodies in Motion

A renowned yogi once called the body a vehicle for the spirit. What freedom there is in shaping that vehicle, in tuning it, in moving it through space and in calling it home. Food tastes better, touch feels more delightful and life looks brighter to a body that has been lovingly exercised.

Good health requires physical motion. Despite this, many people neglect to exercise. They are too busy or unmotivated. They find exercise boring. They are stuck in a rut of inactivity and attached to their own lethargy. Wisely, some turn to personal trainers and instructors to help them bring fitness into their lives. Just as there is no one diet right for everyone, so too there is no single exercise routine that works for everyone's body. Good fitness professionals recognize this and support each client in finding enjoyable, sustainable practices that are perfect for that individual.

Of course, the body requires adequate, pure fuel to keep active and sustain health; nutrition and exercise go hand in hand. It is no surprise, then, that people often turn to their instructors and trainers for advice on how and what to eat. The professionals you will read about next wanted to offer their clients the most accurate, cutting-edge information available, and so they came to Integrative Nutrition. At our school, they learned how to talk to people about food in a way that makes a real difference. They were coached on how to listen and counsel, how to look at their clients from a holistic perspective and help them get lasting results. Our fitness professional graduates are true powerhouses, engaging with clients on every level of health and creating an atmosphere in which these bodies can become truly fit vehicles for the glowing spirits within.

Anita Thompkins

Class of 2004 | New York, NY

Our deepest fear is not that we are inadequate. Our deepest fear is that we are powerful beyond measure.

–Marianne Williamson

Job before Integrative Nutrition: owner of a fitness and wellness center, and before that, Captain in the United States Air Force
Childhood ambition: to be a medical doctor
Favorite snack food: peeled, sweet baby carrots
Favorite healthy food: mushroom and avocado sushi roll
Favorite nutrition book: *Staying Healthy with the Seasons* by Elson Haas, MD
Favorite type of exercise: hatha yoga
Favorite activity outside of work: eating and talking with friends
Craziest thing I've ever done: successfully walking on the ledge of a roof of a 12-story building to work on my balance
Favorite vacation spot: San Francisco, CA
Wildest dream: to have a wellness retreat center in Hawaii or Costa Rica
Proudest moment: becoming a contributing author for *Inspiration to Realization Vol. II*, a book about successful women's strategies for fulfillment
Biggest challenge: fear
Health concerns I've cleared up: acne and knee pain
What I love about Integrative Nutrition: being surrounded by other like-minded individuals
What I love about being a health counselor: seeing transformation in people's lives
What I love about my star client, Lucia: her persistence and consistency

ABOUT MY PRACTICE

Thompkins Fitness & Wellness Center | admin@tfwc.us | www.tfwc.us

My counseling specialty is: assisting clients in developing long-term habits that support them in optimal health, fitness and wellness. I empower clients to change their lives from the inside out through nutrition, exercise and yoga. I assist them in obtaining balance and focus in mind, body and spirit.

My typical client is: female, 30 to 60 years of age, and wants to lose weight, become healthy and take control of her health and well-being. She understands that food can heal, and wants to make the mind-body connection to create balance in her life. I see everything from weight issues, allergies and PMS to diabetes, multiple sclerosis and cancer.

What my clients love about my program: I tailor their holistic health recommendations to what they can do and enjoy. I help them clarify their wants and needs and support them through a "hands-on" approach to wellness.

My favorite juicy question to ask my clients is: If you could do anything in the world, what would it be?

The top three results my clients get from working with me are: unconditional support, achieving their short- and long-term fitness and wellness goals, becoming inspired and motivated, and putting fun back in their lives. My clients lose tons of weight, get off their insulin medication, get pregnant, clear up their skin, and much more. They feel empowered that they can take care of their own health, even if they are dealing with a major illness.

In addition to one-on-one counseling, I also: own and manage a fitness and wellness center, write articles for five magazines, provide lectures on wellness and design specialized programs that include personal training, Pilates and yoga. I also market my teas, The Atina Tea Collection.

What I love about what I do: I love helping others create balance in their lives and achieve their fitness and wellness goals. I love the freedom that I have to create my life with unlimited possibilities. I love the fact that I can be who I am, a woman who marches to her own drum.

How Integrative Nutrition has boosted my business: Since attending the school, I've been working with more and more clients. People from all over, including Ireland and Canada, want to work with me. I've developed an online counseling program, providing materials to use at home and e-mail support from me. I want people everywhere to have access to this work. With in-person and online clients, I can work with about 80 people a month. It's amazing.

My greatest success so far: My client, Lucia, who lost 182 pounds over a two-year period. She has multiple sclerosis and has been able to get off of her diabetes medication and other medications. She is such an inspiration.

In my future, I see myself: empowering people worldwide to aspire to a holistic approach to health and wellness by providing lectures, creating DVDs and audio CDs and publishing articles and books, to support people in their pursuit of wellness. My mission is to inspire people to aspire to greater health, and my vision is worldwide!

CLIENT TESTIMONIAL

Lucia

47 | painter and poet | New York, NY

My parents instilled an interest in art in me from a very early age. I paint and write poetry, and I worked as a video editor until I became disabled. In 1990, I was diagnosed with M.S., with a poor prognosis, perhaps never to walk again. I also suffered from labile diabetes and bipolar disorder. Not content with being relegated to invalidism, I searched out gyms and trainers. Unfortunately, time and again I got a limited workout designed for disabled people, in which I barely progressed at all.

Eventually, good fortune brought me to Anita, who never seemed to see my disability, only my ability. With her guidance, I gained the motivation and encouragement I needed to really begin healing myself. She cleaned up my diet and challenged my body, first with weight training, then walking, and then advanced Pilates. I went from taking insulin five times a day to taking no diabetes medications at all. I have lost more than half my body weight. I am able to walk for more than 20 minutes at a time. I rarely visit the doctors I once visited weekly. They are astounded by my progress and very complimentary.

I no longer crave the foods that would have eventually killed me, and my life is back on track. I look forward to being as confident and competent in the things I love as I can be. Anita is a bright light—encouraging, optimistic and an inspiration. She never discouraged me from trying something new. I am very happy with my progress.

Ken Gibson

Class of 2004 | New York, NY

*The impossible just takes a little longer.
One stroke at a time, one step at a time,
the impossible is easy to achieve. — Tori Murden*

Job before Integrative Nutrition: martial arts instructor, personal trainer and massage therapist
Childhood ambition: to be a carpenter and build my own house
Favorite snack food: big, fresh, warm, slightly gooey cinnamon rolls
Favorite healthy food: coconda from Fiji—a mixed veggie salad with Spanish mackerel, fresh coconut milk, ginger and a little red pepper
Favorite nutrition book: *Nourishing Traditions* by Sally Fallon
Favorite exercise: punching, kicking and grappling
Favorite activity outside of work: spending time with my soon-to-be wife, Christina
What I do to treat myself: see a movie or take a trip
What I do to feel at peace: finish the work at hand, breathe and meditate
Proudest moment: watching my dad hit a home run at a father-son baseball game. Everyone said, "Who's dad is that?" I said, "That's my dad!"
Biggest challenge: killing procrastination
Health concerns I've cleared up: asthma, acne and being overweight
What I love about Integrative Nutrition: They constantly adjust to find the best way to help their students.
What I love about being a health counselor: having clients who make long-term, permanent life changes
What I love about my star client, Mary Clare: She is a caring person who is strong and continues to seek balance in her life.

ABOUT MY PRACTICE

Health Defense | Ken@HealthDefense.org | www.HealthDefense.org

My counseling specialty is: working with people who are taking action to become more balanced. Most are already in some form of martial arts or physical training. I teach them self-defense from the inside out. I believe food and nutrition tools are important tools for living a life of balance.

My typical clients are: busy and need to move themselves higher up their priority list. Most want to lose weight.

The top three results my clients get from working with me are: weight loss, increased energy and healthy tools they can use for the rest of their lives. My clients are amazed at the results they get from working with me. I am able to reach the whole person—physically, mentally and emotionally.

What my clients love about my program: It's tailor-made for them.

My favorite juicy question to ask my clients is: What is the one thing that, if you changed it, would make the biggest difference in your health?

In addition to one-on-one counseling, I also: teach self-defense and fighting skills.

What I love about what I do: seeing people make changes and hearing them say, "Wow, that's easy."

How Integrative Nutrition has boosted my business: Before going to Integrative Nutrition there was a big gap in what I was able to offer. I wanted to learn more about nutrition, but it baffled me because there are so many intimidating theories and people in the field. Now I am no longer afraid of nutrition—I'm an expert in it. My massage school, martial arts school and instruction in personal training never taught me strong business skills. I graduated from Integrative Nutrition with my practice already running and a future growth plan. They taught me how to take all the nutrition information and create a successful business. Now I have a career, not just a job.

My greatest success so far: having clients on both the East coast and West coast. California is my home state, but I also love New York. It's always my dream to be able to travel back home more often. I love that I have the freedom to move around and work wherever I choose.

In the future, I see myself: publishing my first book, traveling more between California and New York and bringing the Health Defense concept to more people.

CLIENT TESTIMONIAL

Mary Clare

37 | owner of martial arts school | New York, NY

I'm a very active person, always learning new skills. I used to take cardio kickboxing class and wanted to take it to the next level, so I began studying martial arts. Now I own a studio. I train a minimum of seven hours a week and recently added karate and rock-climbing to my skills. I met Ken when he came to teach a class at my studio. He's a very positive person and a very good martial artist. I hired him as my counselor.

I'd just had a bad break-up with a boyfriend, wasn't eating right and didn't like how my business was going. This was unusual because I'm a really positive person who stays on top of her responsibilities. I didn't like the way I looked or felt. Plus I was going out on the town and drinking with friends a lot. I didn't realize how tired and depressed that was making me.

I liked Ken's holistic approach. He helped me see the importance of putting energy into all areas of my life, not just business, so I could feel more balanced. I started having better breakfasts instead of decaf and a muffin. He got me eating a lot more greens. I do a better job now of going to the grocery store on weekends so that I can cook for myself. These changes gave me the momentum to not drink, and that helped everything else fall into place. Now I have more energy and can run my business better. I've lost some weight and look a lot better, too. I'm grateful to Ken for his support and persistence, and I'm looking forward to a future that includes a very profitable business and a great relationship!

Debra Duby

Class of 2004 | Stamford, CT

Do or do not.
There is no try.
—Yoda, Star Wars

Job before Integrative Nutrition: owner of a personal training business
Childhood ambition: to be an Olympic athlete
Favorite snack food: Green and Black's Organic 70% Dark Chocolate with fresh peanut butter
Favorite healthy food: sliced baked yams, sliced baked green apples and pecan halves with agave nectar, sea salt and cinnamon
Favorite nutrition book: *Food and Healing* by Annemarie Colbin, PhD
Favorite exercise: strength training
Favorite activity outside of work: dancing
What I do to treat myself: take a nap or get a massage
What I do to feel at peace: hang out with my husband, sit in the sun or drink a hot beverage by myself
Wildest dream: to be a part of a global effort to improve the health of people and the planet
Proudest moment: standing at the starting line in front of the ocean at my first triathlon
Biggest challenge: loving and accepting myself for who I am and who I am not
Health concerns I've cleared up: a seven-year habit of eating in the middle of the night, phantom stomach pains and sugar binges
What I love about Integrative Nutrition: learning that great health is achieved through a combination of the food we eat and a life that we love
What I love about being a health counselor: It is an honor to partner with people in their quest towards living a happy and healthy life.
What I love about my star client, Shamus: He puts the pedal to the metal, while enjoying the process.

ABOUT MY PRACTICE

Soul Salad Ltd. | info@soulsaladltd.com | www.soulsaladltd.com

My counseling specialty is: helping people increase their energy by discovering which foods sustain them, which exercise program works best for their body type and what lifestyle behaviors need modification. Our physical condition and mental outlook are mutually dependent on one another. Continuing to refine this relationship is the key to realizing our potential as individuals.

My typical client is: highly motivated, ready to take action and committed to the process. Many of my clients are high-level, proactive people like CEOs, COOs, actors, medical doctors and attorneys.

The top three results my clients get from working with me are: clarity, motivation and confidence. They meet their health goals, but the results go deeper than that. They gain new passion for their lives and futures.

Why I combine health counseling and personal training: I went to Integrative Nutrition because I knew that fitness was multifaceted, and I wanted to offer even greater benefits to my clients through food. My combined program includes strength, cardio, and flexibility training, as well as individualized food recommendations and personal counseling. The counseling piece is important. My goal is to give clients lifelong, permanent results, and in order for changes to be sustainable, we have to see clearly what is going on in their lives.

My favorite juicy question to ask my clients is: Are you a fast or slow eater? How they answer this question tells me almost everything I need to know.

What my clients love about my program: personalized direction coupled with unconditional support. I give my clients a foundation for self-confidence. When people feel empowered around their health, they are unstoppable!

In addition to one-on-one counseling, I also: offer personal training, group programs, corporate programs, food and fitness group vacations, and makeovers.

What I love about what I do: There is nothing more rewarding than working with people towards goals that will affect the quality of their lives.

My greatest success so far: Discovering how to align holistic living with the goals of corporate America. As employees improve their health, they are able to think more clearly and increase the quality of their work. Through a few key quality-of-life changes, businesses are able to gain a competitive edge and improve the bottom line.

In the future, I see: limitless opportunities for me to inspire people to live a life they love—in my family, in my friendships and in my business. I cannot think of a better way to spend my time.

CLIENT TESTIMONIAL

Shamus

42 | hedge fund COO | New Canaan, CT

I have a high-pressure, fast-paced job that keeps me going all day. I also have a very active life with my three kids. We ski in the winters and water ski, jet-ski and swim in the summers. I coach their sports teams, and we are active together in our community. I noticed that my metabolism had slowed, and I was getting out of shape. I was eating what was comfortable, fast and easy. With my busy schedule I would skip breakfast, blow through lunch, eat dinner at 9:00 p.m. and snack a lot. All of a sudden the kids were tiring me out. I said, nope, that's not going to happen to me, and started looking for help with my diet and exercise.

Debra turned out to be exactly the right person to work with. Now my family and I eat organic produce, meat, eggs, butter and whole grain pastas as our main staples. I try to eat smarter breakfasts, cut out unhealthy foods and have a variety of foods for lunch. I train with Debra two days a week, doing cardio, legs and abs. She's awesome and so detailed. She has a clear plan and explains how the exercises tie together so I know why I'm doing them.

I'm in much better shape now, no question. My waist has come in a couple of inches, and I'm overall more toned and built. I feel better about what I'm eating and the process of training. My goal is to keep my life going at the pace I'm going. If I want to be skiing with my kids when I'm 60, I need to eat right and stay in shape. I think Debra will be a big part of that.

7

Supporting Families

There is a deep pleasure in the simple act of sharing food with others. A generosity is inspired, a gratitude for the food is cultivated and a kinship is nurtured.

How sad, then, that in our fast-food, fast-moving society it is uncommon for families to join together at mealtime. At Integrative Nutrition, we call for this to change. We believe that families who eat together, stay together. And we encourage the preparation of home-cooked meals. When fresh, whole foods are created with tender hands for beloved partners and children, the health of all is supported. Coming together to enjoy this food promotes bonding and communication, and by eating the same foods family members tend to have increased relatedness. After all, the same nutritional components are becoming the building blocks for each person's cells, blood, brains and thoughts.

Many parents attend Integrative Nutrition and report on the miraculous results of such practices on their family systems. They tell us that raising their kids on whole, natural foods is easier than some think, and that their children are calmer, stronger and more focused because of it. Our students also tell us that their partnerships are bolstered when clean food is prepared and shared with significant others.

The graduates in this chapter are working with mothers and fathers, couples and children to reinforce the importance of family mealtime and to teach the benefits of rearing our next generation on good food and better principles of healthy lifestyle. The fortunate couples and families who rely on these counselors are creating homes in which healthy bodies and relationships bloom, setting a precedent for the ideal future of American families that we here at Integrative Nutrition envision.

Pam Pinto

Class of 2004 | Thomaston, CT

We have not inherited the Earth from our fathers; we are borrowing it from our children. -Lester Brown

Job before Integrative Nutrition: trade show sales coordinator
Childhood ambition: to make my mark on the world!
Favorite snack food: hummus and cucumbers
Favorite healthy food: sautéed rainbow chard with tahini sauce or spicy brown rice with beans
Favorite nutrition book: *Fast Food Nation* by Eric Schlosser
Favorite type of exercise: walking
Favorite activity outside of work: home-school field trips with my children
What I do to treat myself: a long, hot shower
What I do to feel at peace: meditate
Wildest dream: to have a best-selling book that touches millions
Proudest moment: becoming a mother
Biggest challenge: giving my children a healthy environment
Health concerns I've cleared up: candida, sugar cravings, hormone imbalances and PMS
What I love about Integrative Nutrition: It gave me the ability to "feel the fear and do it anyway."
What I love about being a health counselor: educating many other people, which in turn helps to create social change
What I love about my star client, Bernadette: how she has stuck to her commitment to making healthy lifestyle changes, and how she puts her children first

ABOUT MY PRACTICE

Mindful Mama | lora@mindfulmama.com | www.mindfulmama.com

My counseling specialty is: pregnancy and fertility issues. When I work with a client I help her to figure out the best food choices for her pregnancy, including foods to fuel her baby's development at different stages in the womb. I also help her to find specific times to express her creativity. Pregnancy is such a creative time—I really help to nurture that.

My typical client is: a woman who wants to make healthy choices as she transitions into motherhood, physically and mentally.

My favorite juicy question to ask my clients is: As a mother, what will you gain and what will you have to leave behind?

What my clients love about my program: Working on the specifics of health and nutrition during pregnancy, as well as getting into the magical mysteries of birth.

The top three results my clients get from working with me are: mindful eating during pregnancy and into the future, improved body image and feeling empowered to make the best choices for themselves. My pregnant clients report feeling more energized and more in control. Clients who come in looking to get pregnant often begin regular ovulation and menstruation, and then conceive. Others are able to go into in-vitro fertilization feeling more empowered and knowledgeable.

In addition to one-on-one counseling, I also: teach childbirth preparation and support laboring couples as a doula. I am also going to school so I can further serve people as a registered nurse.

Why I work with moms-to-be: I get really jazzed up by helping women figure out what it takes to become healthy and receptive to new life. I'm very into women feeling empowered, so that no matter what happens with trying to get pregnant or with their birth plans, they feel aware, at peace and in control. I also value the idea that we create our children's futures by what we feed them and ourselves. The work I do is not just for my women clients, but for their whole families. I'm helping to affect future generations.

What I love about what I do: I get to work for myself. I get to work in the service of others. I get to learn about the healing powers of food. I get to problem solve.

My greatest success so far: I worked with a woman who was thinking about having a child, but she had not had her period for over a year. Just one week after our first session she got her period! We finished our sessions a few months ago, and I just got an e-mail saying that she is pregnant. Life is dynamic and amazing!

In the future, I see myself: as a midwife and health counselor. I will help babies to be born and I will help women to be born as mothers—guiding them holistically through issues of nutrition, health and the joys of self-discovery.

CLIENT TESTIMONIAL

Jennifer

33 | stay-at-home mom/HR professional | Brooklyn, NY

Raising a toddler is pretty hectic, but family life is a priority for me. I think there is no better feeling than the love that one gets from one's child—it's indescribable. Becoming pregnant made me start thinking about my health differently. Suddenly there was another person depending on my body, and that prompted me to make changes. I knew this was a lifetime commitment to my own health because I want to live as long as I can so I can take care of and enjoy this child.

One of my goals for my program was to get out of bad eating habits, like eating candy, chocolate and ice cream. I introduced a lot more vegetables into my diet and cut down on sugar and started drinking plenty of water. These simple food changes gave me more energy, fewer headaches, fewer mood swings, less constipation and a more positive attitude. Lora helped me to relax, take small, achievable steps towards my goals and accept myself. She saw what I was capable of and helped me to achieve a lot without being hard on myself. It was a real pleasure working with her.

Lora supported me in every way through my pregnancy—giving me teas, remedies and exercises for back pain, sleeplessness and other ailments of pregnancy. At the birth, Lora was fantastic—so loving, so giving and adjusting to my needs. Having her there made the birth process much easier for me. Lora is a wonderful guiding presence in my life—there just aren't enough good things to say about her.

Uri Feiner

Class of 2005 | New York, NY

You miss 100% of the shots you don't take. — Wayne Gretzky

Job before Integrative Nutrition: computer consultant
Childhood ambition: to rule the world
Favorite snack food: goat and sheep's milk yogurt with sunflower seeds, raw cacao beans and agave nectar
Favorite healthy food: dandelion greens and garlic sautéed in olive oil
Favorite nutrition book: *Healing With Whole Foods* by Paul Pitchford
Favorite type of exercise: skiing in the mountains of Vermont
Favorite activity outside of work: cycling through the streets of New York
What I do to treat myself: go to my favorite cafe in Greenwich Village
What I do to feel at peace: dedicate one day a week to doing absolutely nothing
Wildest dream: to transform the perspective on healthy marriage in America
Proudest moment: receiving front-page news coverage by the media
Biggest challenge: overcoming perfectionism
Health concerns I've cleared up: severe asthma and allergies, weak immune system, low energy and caffeine dependency
What I love about Integrative Nutrition: its nondogmatic philosophy and extraordinary support to get out there to effect change
What I love about being a health counselor: watching my clients transform their lives
What I love about my star clients, Dave and Lana: They are open, eager and committed to integrating new habits into their lives.

ABOUT MY PRACTICE

Thriving Health | info@thrivinghealth.com | www.thrivinghealth.com

My counseling specialty is: helping couples create amazing relationships by integrating better eating habits and making gradual lifestyle changes together.

My typical client is: a couple who wants to maximize their energy, manage their weight, eliminate cravings for sugar and caffeine, and clear up digestive issues, allergies and skin problems. They need a lot of support around how to help each other to be healthy. I work with them on communication skills, empathizing and supporting each other. By helping each other improve their relationship to food, their relationship to one another improves accordingly.

What my clients love about my program: being challenged, with compassion and total support, to get to the bottom of their health issues. They also love learning to "read" what their body truly needs. We laugh a lot, and there's an emphasis on fun. Eating together becomes a source of nourishment instead of a source of stress.

My favorite juicy question to ask my clients is: How's your relationship going these days? (to each member of the couple, with the other present)

The top three results my clients get from working with me are: high energy and good sleep without dependence on sugar, caffeine or drugs, plus getting down to their ideal weight without using willpower. As a couple gets healthier, they become much more respectful and understanding of each other. There is less battle and more partnership.

In addition to couples counseling, I also: run group programs, lead corporate wellness programs and lecture widely. I'm currently working on two books.

Why I work with couples: It's hard to have successful relationships and family lives in today's busy culture. My wife Corie and I want to help turn that around. We are in a highly sustainable marriage. We have a shared vision and goals around food, health and well-being. Part of our commitment to one another is to support each other's health. Because of the happiness and success in my own marriage, I want to help other couples.

What I love about what I do: empowering my clients to take charge of their health and watching their health problems melt away. My energy is highest after a full day of seeing clients—they are so inspiring. I'm thrilled and amazed to have a career that fits all my passions, and that I can share with my partner, Corie, who is also a health counselor and who runs the practice with me.

My greatest success so far: becoming a requested lecturer in prominent learning institutions, and discovering that my career as a health counselor, which I love, is as lucrative as my old career in computer networking.

In the future, I see myself: doing lots of public speaking, running large seminars, writing many articles and books and, ultimately, inspiring millions of people to lead happier and healthier lives and relationships.

CLIENT TESTIMONIAL

Dave

34 | instructor and doctoral student, history | Brooklyn, NY

I had spent a decade gaining weight and had just started walking five and a half miles a day to manage it. More and more I was becoming concerned that I didn't want to die at 50. I love my wife Lana and I want us to grow old together. Uri has helped me to find my own motivation to eat healthier, instead of following a set of rules.

The changes in my diet are like night and day. I lost 20 pounds in four months. I gave up caffeine and am less tired. Lana and I do a lot of cooking at home together now, and we eat together more than in the past. Someday I may thank Uri for saving my life. Right now I can thank him for helping me to help myself. I'm looking forward to being healthier, appreciating Lana and being alive for a good, long time.

Lana

27 | arts manager and graduate student | Brooklyn, NY

I knew about how to be healthier, but with my busy life I found a lot of excuses. I had quite a problem with eating too much sugar and didn't know how to handle it. Uri helped Dave and me to view wellness in a completely different way. Now we enjoy cooking together, walking together and other healthy activities. I'm cooking more and eating in a balanced way. I've really conquered my sugar addiction and have lots of little things that make me feel better, like drinking more water and doing yoga.

After getting out of the army Dave put on a lot of weight, but now he's healthier and uncovering that gorgeous man with all the muscles. It's exciting! The number one thing for me is that Dave and I are in this together. If he is healthier and will live longer, then I will be happier too.

In Schools and Communities

A ll around us there is need for more clean air, clean water, green spaces, affordable health insurance and access to high-quality food. The leaders who have emerged to teach on these subjects are a noble lot, and Integrative Nutrition graduates are among those honorable people serving our communities.

We have found that when the value of healthy diet and lifestyle is taught to the people in community groups and schools, these organizations are permanently altered. The cohesiveness and energy generated by such education touches person after person within the organization, who in turn impact people without, creating a ripple effect of positive, dynamic change. Many schools continue to feed our growing children processed, sugary junk, despite the proof that this is harmful to them. Working with schools to provide nourishing lunches for kids, forming vocal advocacy groups, holding local conferences, providing health counseling to the disadvantaged and collaborating with city councils, religious groups and other organizations are some of the ways in which our graduates are reaching out to create change on a macro level.

The alumni whose stories follow operate thriving businesses, while altering society. Their strength, commitment and passion are inspirational. Every day they are fueled by recognizing their place in the formation of a brighter, healthier future. Perhaps reading their stories will call out to your greater virtues, and stir you to take that step from the personal to the communal, and from there, to the universal.

Susan Rubin

Class of 1999 | Chappaqua, NY

You can do anything if you have enthusiasm. Enthusiasm is the yeast that makes your hopes rise to the stars.

—Henry Ford

Job before Integrative Nutrition: dentist
Childhood ambition: world leader
Favorite snack food: Ronnybrook Farm coconut yogurt sprinkled with Schokinag European drinking chocolate
Favorite healthy food: carrot and burdock kinpira
Favorite kitchen tool: my immersion blender
Favorite exercise: yoga
My favorite activity outside of work: beading with my kids
Favorite vacation spot: Key West
Craziest thing I've ever done: traveled the country making a documentary
Wildest dream: to travel the world with my family
Proudest moment: seeing how much my kids enjoyed harvesting 30 pounds of lettuce from a local organic garden
Biggest challenge: raising three daughters in a crazy, mixed-up world
What I love about Integrative Nutrition: It gave me the education I was looking for—one that helps me make a real difference.
Health concerns I've cleared up: low energy—I don't use an alarm clock to get up anymore. I pop out of bed eager to greet the day.
What I love about being a health counselor: the freedom, flexibility and creativity. It's great to be my own boss!
What I love about my star client, Denise: She had the courage to step outside of the box and re-create her own life.

ABOUT MY PRACTICE

A Better Way Holistic Health | abetterwayhhc@aol.com | www.drsusanrubin.com | www.angrymoms.org

My counseling specialty is: working with busy moms who have had a health wake-up call. As a dentist I used to speak in schools about the damage junk food and sugar were doing to kids' health. As a counselor over the last six years I have helped thousands of parents and children change their diets and get healthier. It's amazing and very rewarding.

My typical client is: a busy mom with lots of stress and not enough time, who wants to make things better for herself and her family.

What my clients love about my program: It's different from anything they've ever tried before. After working with me, they never need to go on another "diet" again.

My favorite juicy question to ask my clients is: What would you do if you knew you couldn't fail?

The top three results my clients get from working with me are: less stress and more freedom around food; more fun in their lives; better energy and appearance, for both themselves and their kids.

In addition to one-on-one counseling, I also: teach cooking classes, facilitate group programs for adults, kids and organizations, run a nonprofit coalition to improve school food in my county and raise national awareness about the importance of feeding children healthy foods in school.

How I am creating change in schools: My junk food awareness program has been implemented in many schools across the country. I show policy-makers and advocates how they can make simple changes like giving kids more water, locally grown fresh vegetables and foods without dyes. I am also making a documentary with another Integrative Nutrition graduate, Amy Kalafa, called *Two Angry Moms.* We interview food service vendors, teachers, health experts, politicians, parents and officials from the USDA and FDA to discover what has gone wrong with our National School Lunch Program and to provide workable solutions.

What I love about what I do: being a witness to the positive transformation of others. Most of us already know what we should be eating; we just need support and guidance. Our healthcare system is faltering, and the solution is to reconnect with our food, to get back to the basics of eating well. I love helping my clients through this process. This is what the conversation always comes back to—with clients, with parents, with advocates—eating simpler, healthier food that is close to home.

My greatest success so far: The Westchester Coalition for Better School Food held our first major conference this spring. Participants included the American Cancer Society, the American Diabetes Association, the Westchester Department of Health and the American Heart Association. All these major organizations contacted me and asked if they could participate. It's very exciting!

In the future, I see myself: as a leader in a growing national movement of better school food and empowered moms who know how to feed themselves and their families. We're gonna take back our health!

CLIENT TESTIMONIAL

Denise

39 | travel writer | Europe

My career, family life and lifestyle are very different now than before I met Susan. I was a stressed-out lawyer turned stay-at-home mom. I didn't want to return to the life of a lawyer, and I didn't want to stay at home without additional intellectual stimulation. Although I generally have a good sense of humor and love of life, I found myself taking antidepressants, and then a sleep agent to counter the sleep disorder caused by the antidepressants. It was a mess. Realizing that my life was out of control, I decided to seek help.

My diet was junk. I was eating lots of processed, prepared foods and white-flour–based foods. I started eating whole grains, fresh green vegetables and simple, organic, unprocessed foods with no additives. My emotional and physical health improved substantially. I lost weight. I now have no depression. I sleep well. I feel healthy. My life is more wholesome and balanced. Everything good stems from that.

I used to be very invested in financial success and recognition, but through my work with Susan I became most committed to peace, happiness and the health of my family. Today I am living my dream of a life overseas as a travel writer. I moved with my family from the United States to Europe, where the pace of life is slower and where I can more easily live in harmony with my deepest values. Susan helped me to see that those steps were in easy reach and to make my journey one step at a time. I'm grateful to her for being the catalyst for these powerful changes in my life and for believing in me.

Diana Patton

Class of 2005 | Toledo, OH

Joy is prayer - joy is strength - joy is love- joy is a net of love by which you can catch souls. — Mother Teresa

Job before Integrative Nutrition: diversity director for major corporation

Childhood ambition: to become the first black woman Supreme Court Justice

Favorite snack food: raw nuts and raisins

Favorite healthy food: green salad with avocado, almonds, cranberries and tons of vegetables

Favorite nutrition book: *Digestive Wellness* by Elizabeth Lipski, PhD, CCN

Favorite type of exercise: spinning, running or stretching

Favorite activity outside of work: playing on the swings with my children or one-on-one basketball with my husband

Favorite vacation spot: Maui

Biggest risk I've taken: quitting my corporate job making six figures to start my holistic health business, and I am sure glad I did!

Wildest dream: to speak to a crowd of millions about my passion for holistic living

Proudest moment: presenting the first Damon A. Pinskey Memorial Scholarship to a student at my old high school, in memory of my brother

Biggest challenge: passing the Ohio State Bar Examination

Health concerns I've cleared up: poor digestion, yeast issues and low energy

What I love about Integrative Nutrition: its drive to stay true to what is right, cutting-edge, wholesome and good

What I love about being a health counselor: running my own company, and meeting people right where they are and helping them love their lives

What I love about my star client, Letty: her spirit and passion to want to live a better life

ABOUT MY PRACTICE

Equilibria, LLC | diana@equilibriabydiana.com | www.equilibriabydiana.com

My counseling specialty is: purpose building, time management, food and fitness for body and life.

My typical clients: lead very busy lives and sometimes have "Type A" personalities. They have difficulty getting to sleep, crave sugar and caffeine for energy and have gastrointestinal issues such as irritable bowel syndrome, acid reflux or Crohn's disease. They long for the day when they can eat easy, healthy food and lead a balanced life with sustained energy from the time they wake up until the time they go to sleep.

What my clients love about my program: They feel very comfortable, accepted and loved from session one. They especially love the one-on-one contact and encouraging atmosphere. A lot of them say that they love the laughter and the light, spiritual quality that they experience while they ease into their new way of living, eating and thinking. Oh, and we must not forget that they really love the weight loss!

My favorite juicy question to ask my clients is: What is your deepest, most sought-after desire, and why isn't that desire a reality in your life now?

The top three results my clients get from working with me are: a renewed belief that they are a treasured gift from God; increased energy and a zeal for life; weight loss and an overall fit feeling.

In addition to one-on-one counseling, I also: conduct corporate programs, athletic life programs and group cleansing courses, and operate a nonprofit organization for teens. I have a large network and a determined, passionate nature, so I've been able to share my knowledge with many influential people including high-level entrepreneurial women, women athletes in Canada, and doctors and nurses at a local integrative medicine center. I also teach churches and other nonprofit organizations about holistic health and help people understand Ohio's Health Freedom Law.

The greatest difference I've made in my community so far: I've had the privilege of teaching teens at a local high school for pregnant teenagers and mothers. I've planted positive seeds for the future for these young ladies and their children by teaching them about the core fundamentals of time management, healthy food acceptance and the art of loving themselves. My team has created a city-wide event in which 10,000 teens will learn to experience health from a body, mind and spirit perspective and will be mentored by 1,000 local leaders.

My greatest success so far: being awarded for my efforts in holistic health and for my community focus by the Greater Toledo Urban League of Young Professionals and by the American Heart Association as an ambassador for Women's Heart Health.

In the future, I see myself: publishing a book, expanding my business nationally, opening a whole food and juice cuisine restaurant, and completing construction on the Equilibria Life Center as a place for healing, education and inspiration.

CLIENT TESTIMONIAL

Letty

34 | mom | Sylvania, OH

Being a good wife and mother is very important to me. I'm dedicated to raising my three beautiful children, to taking care of our home and to doing my volunteer work. So when I had health problems and could not be there as much for my family, it really affected how I felt about myself. I'd gone through two heart surgeries due to arrhythmia and tachycardia episodes. The doctors put me on so many medications that I had to have my gallbladder taken out. Then they diagnosed me with endometriosis. For two years my stomach felt off all the time. I had heart palpitations and nausea. I lost twenty pounds. Some days I couldn't get out of bed. I felt so sick, and the doctors couldn't help me.

When I went to see Diana for a consultation, she made me feel comfortable and took time to explain what was going on in my body. She gave me hope that things could get better. I made changes like reducing fast food, red meat and soda, and eating green vegetables. Within a month or two my stomach pain and heart palpitations really diminished. My energy level and mood changed completely. I'm healthy enough now that my doctors have taken me off of or reduced all my medications. I've got a healthy glow!

Working with Diana, I've really gotten to know my body and to understand myself spiritually. She helped me to see how I carry my stress and to let go of my fears of death and illness. Now I can play with my children without being exhausted, and I take time to garden, walk my dog and enjoy nature. The thought that I'm not going to be sick for the rest of my life makes me look at my future in such a different way.

Linda Hazel

Class of 2005 | Queens, NY

Thou hast made us for thyself, and we are happy only when we dwell in Thee.

— *St. Augustine*

Job before Integrative Nutrition: educator and entrepreneur
Childhood ambition: to teach
Favorite snack food: hull-less popcorn with white cheddar cheese
Favorite healthy food: collard green quiche
Favorite nutrition book: *Eat Right 4 Your Type* by Peter D'Adamo, ND
Favorite exercise: walking in the outdoors
Favorite activity outside of work: traveling to the Caribbean, South America, Europe or Africa to meet other people interested in health and spirituality
Craziest thing I've ever done: start a business with only $140
Favorite vacation spot: Bermuda
Wildest dream: to be known as the "red hot holistic health diva"
Proudest moment: being nationally recognized for my work on safe drinking water for our communities
Biggest challenge: getting the message out about health problems caused by lead in our water and by other environmental concerns
Health concerns I've cleared up: Hodgkins lymphoma, pancreatic cancer, colitis and nerve pain
What I love about Integrative Nutrition: It gave me the tools to present my nutritional knowledge in diverse ways and in a professional manner.
What I love about being a health counselor: the pleasure of working with my clients and seeing their personal triumphs
What I love about my star client, Edna: She is a dear friend.

ABOUT MY PRACTICE

A Betterway Holistic Health Counseling | abetterwayhhc@yahoo.com

My counseling specialty is: helping adults make a smooth transition into retirement. I have special expertise in cancer survival and spiritual development.

My typical client is: in late middle age and wants to transition into retirement on a minimum of medications, and is in good physical and mental shape. Most are accomplished African American business professionals and leaders from schools, city boards and churches.

What my clients love about my program: mastering their individual dietary needs and concerns and gaining energy from proper nutrition. Many like working with me because they see that I am successful and healthy. I am 65 and in great shape! People ask me how I've done it, and they want a little of what I've got.

The top three results my clients get from working with me are: appropriate weight loss or gain, pain relief and a great feeling of well-being.

My favorite juicy question to ask my clients is: What's new and good with you?

In addition to one-on-one counseling, I also: designed and currently teach public programs providing nutritional guidance to groups in my community through a grant from the NYC Parks Department Shape Up program. I sit on city boards, including the national drinking water advisory committee, to rewrite laws on lead and copper in water in schools. As an evangelist in the Roman Catholic Church, I work with priests and other religious leaders at retreats and healing circles.

What I love about what I do: the high level of affection and trust my clients share with me, and seeing them improve and meet their goals. They are all doing so well, it's wonderful.

How I am making a difference in my community: I am very involved in my community and known for what I do. I have worked with the Chamber of Commerce, the Office of Black Ministry for the Diocese of Brooklyn and Queens, and the Presidents Club of the public schools' PTA. My mission is to touch as many lives as I can. I am especially concerned about diet issues in the African American community. I try to help people in poorer neighborhoods get access to healthier foods in their local communities.

My greatest success so far: one of my clients, a city councilman, advocating for my grant from the NYC Parks Department. It's also just fantastic to have my own business. I've been working for nonprofits and serving people my whole life. What a pleasure to discover that the caring and expertise that I've been giving away for free, people are very willing to pay for. I am making plenty of money and have plenty of clients.

In the future, I see myself: having many speaking opportunities to share this important work with populations in need of nutritional and dietary guidance.

CLIENT TESTIMONIAL

Edna

58 | teacher | New York, NY

I've known Linda for 20 years. I was a teacher at a day care center she used to run. Even back then she was concerned about the health of children in our community, teaching them yoga and serving no sugar or food additives. Over the years Linda shared a lot with me about how I could improve my health by what I eat. When she got her education at Integrative Nutrition, I made a commitment to work with her for six months. I was overweight and getting tired more easily than I should have been.

I wasn't a person who ate a bad diet, but I did not know there were certain foods I should avoid. I learned that wheat is not good for me personally. I also cut out white rice and white starches. I started eating more green vegetables, fresh fruits, chicken and fish. I've had a lot success eating more according to my blood type. With Linda's help I've also added walking to my life, a mile a day, even though I have a physical disability. I lost about 20 pounds, and I feel better for sure! I have much more stamina to do the things I enjoy.

I found Linda very warm, attentive, approachable and knowledgeable. I think these qualities help her work well with people from all walks of life. She is very concerned about the health of the African American community. We are plagued with diabetes, heart problems and other diseases, which are all related to weight and diet. Linda has done a lot to raise the consciousness of people in this community, especially those who have not been used to paying attention to nutrition. She is so passionate and willing to share. I'm grateful for her compassion and concern for my community, my family and me.

Healing Oppression

It is a natural function of the human mind to divide and categorize, to label and judge. But when fear is present, bigotry stems forth. Sexism, racism, ageism, homophobia, religious bias, classism—all these forms of hatred corrode the health and the heart. When we are slighted by other's prejudiced views and turn those feelings against ourselves, we dampen our true natures. We may weaken and limit ourselves and fail to pursue our dreams. Stress, pain, loneliness and disease abound.

Integrative Nutrition's holistic approach to healing a sick or weak body requires supporting clients to abandon such false, cruel beliefs that have been imposed by parents, teachers, religions, the media or other institutions. Brown rice and kale may delight the digestive tract and promise rich nutrients, but complete and vibrant health is only possible through the self-care that comes from self-love and self-acceptance.

The Integrative Nutrition graduates in this section are working with clients to address the sexism, racism and other forms of discrimination that have compromised their well-being. As these clients acknowledge and release the past, they experience lightness. Their symptoms are relieved, their energies restored and their moods improved. One by one, they begin to create new futures for themselves, connecting our country and our world to a future in which health, happiness, kinship and love will prosper.

Kiu Eubanks

Class of 2002 | Durham, NC

The fruit of the Spirits is love, joy, peace, patience, kindness, goodness, faithfulness, gentleness and self-control.

-The Bible

Job before Integrative Nutrition: therapist

Childhood ambition: to be a writer

Favorite snack food: pecans and raisins in applesauce

Favorite healthy food: black beans, brown rice and veggies

Favorite nutrition book: *Integrative Nutrition* by Joshua Rosenthal, MScEd

Favorite exercise: working out on the elliptical trainer

Favorite activity outside of work: going out dancing

What I do to treat myself: get massages from Chinese Tui-Na practitioners

What I do to feel at peace: get adequate sleep, stop moving, read, or lay down under my orgone blanket

Wildest dream: to win 10 million dollars and live in the tropics

Proudest moment: the birth of my daughter

Biggest challenge: a persistent penchant for sweets

Health concerns that I've cleared up by changing my diet: hormonal imbalances and PMS

What I love about Integrative Nutrition: the authentic communication

What I love about being a health counselor: witnessing transformation

What I love about my star client, Angela: She is focused, motivated and kind.

ABOUT MY PRACTICE

Synthesis Holistic Services | kiusmith@fastmail.fm | www.synthesisholistic.com

My counseling specialty is: self-care and stress reduction for women. My clinical training in psychology helps me to thoroughly address the impact of stress and emotions on food choice, as well as any traumatic events, depression, anxiety or body image issues. I help clients understand the underlying reasons why they don't take care of themselves well.

My typical client is: exhausted, slightly overweight, intelligent, multitalented and nurturing. She wants to be well-rested, vibrant, able to set limits and willing to take time for her own joy. Most of my clients are African American women from communities where there is pressure to be a superwoman who takes care of everyone else—her family, her church, her community. This is okay, until it becomes detrimental to a woman's health. The health concerns I see most often are obesity, high blood pressure, diabetes, high cholesterol and some heart disease.

What are the major social and health challenges that your clients face?: The major illnesses in the African American community could all be improved with better food choices and less stress. There is a need here for healthy food and holistic healing, but it can be a challenge. Holistic lifestyle is becoming a luxury item; healthy food and services are often overpriced. Working families need affordable access to health food stores, organic restaurants and holistic services, without having to leave their own neighborhoods.

What my clients love about my program: African American women can be hesitant to come into a therapeutic situation that seems vague or purposeless. They want to know that this isn't just sitting around talking—that it has the power to help them meet their goals in concrete ways. That's what I give them. They see that I'm from where they are from and have been where they've been, and that I can help.

My favorite juicy question to ask my clients: When did you stop making care of yourself a priority?

The top three results my clients get from working with me are: weight loss through good food choices, mental clarity and energy. Eating well transforms multiple layers of their lives: food choice, time management, saying no and self-love.

In addition to one-on-one counseling, I've also: written a 30 Stress & Self-Care Actions program, available as a workbook. I present this program at seminars and at private pampering parties. I am also a doctoral student in counseling psychology.

What I love about what I do: It resonates with me as a key component of my divine purpose on earth. It is more than a job. It is the vehicle to manifest my consciousness. Integrative Nutrition showed me how to manifest my vision, and to believe in possibilities without limitation. It opened the door to my own healing, and taught me how to do that work for others.

My greatest success so far: Providing hundreds of women with insight, information and pampering through my beauty and wellness events.

In my future I see: a super luxurious, yet economically accessible wellness center and spa. It's called Luscious.

CLIENT TESTIMONIAL

Angela

40 | quality assurance manager | Cary, NC

At the time I met Kiu I was working long, stressful hours. I was sitting most of the day, not getting to the gym, and bringing home fast food for my teenage daughter and me. I wasn't sleeping well, waking up at night anxious about work. On top of this, my cholesterol was high and I wanted to reduce it without medication.

The most important thing I learned from working with Kiu was how to value the importance of taking care of myself. She tasked me to make commitments to myself like meditating in the mornings, not doing work after a certain time, and taking time out for myself, like reading or walking in the park. This made a big difference. Kiu also helped me plan my weekly meals, introduced me to the health food store, and gave me healthy snacks, teas and a great cookbook. Now that I am not working as much, I have time to cook more. I'm having more fish, whole wheat and oatmeal, using less salt and sugar, and loving my vegetables, especially a healthy version of collard greens.

My stress level is much lower since working with Kiu. I trust that my work will get done. Having time to go to the gym feels great and is helping me get in shape. I'm going to bed between 9:30 and 10:00 and sleeping through the night. I'm looking forward to a long, healthy life, and am excited to see how my new habits bring down my cholesterol and help me avoid heart disease. Having Kiu there to help me with my plan was much easier than trying to do this alone. I'm grateful to her for showing me the path of renewal.

Darshana Weil

Class of 1997 | San Francisco, CA

Be the change you wish to see in the world. —Gandhi

Job before Integrative Nutrition: professional musical theater actress
Childhood ambition: to be a professional actress and also run a holistic healing center
Favorite snack food: dried bananas, not banana chips but the dried fruit—yum!
Favorite healthy food: greens, greens and more greens
Favorite nutrition book: *The Yoga of Eating* by Charles Eisenstein
Favorite exercise: long power walks in nature
Favorite activity outside of work: yoga
Favorite vacation spot: any mountain
What I do to feel at peace: sing or spend time with my husband and friends
Wildest dream: to live in another country very different from the US and learn a different way of being in the world through the culture and the people
Proudest moment: any moment when I know deep inside that what I'm doing is the right thing for my spirit and soul
Biggest challenge: time management—I want to do too many things!
Health concerns I've cleared up: poor digestion, irregular and painful periods, mood swings, knee problems and obsession with my weight and body image
What I love about Integrative Nutrition: its radical yet completely simple viewpoints on diet and a balanced life
What I love about being a health counselor: being with people and watching them grow and become more excited
What I love about my star client, Susan: her amazement, enjoyment and enthusiasm every time we added a new food to her diet

ABOUT MY PRACTICE

Fruition Women's Health | www.fruitionhealth.com

My counseling specialty is: working with women just like me. I know they will heal because they come to me with the same issues that I used to suffer from. I am great at staying present with my clients. We work in the moment, one step at a time.

My typical client is: a woman who struggles with negative thinking about herself and her body. She is uncomfortable with her weight and puts foods into two categories: good and bad. She may have digestive issues, PMS, migraines, hormonal imbalances, etc. She does not want to feel deprived when she eats. She wants a healthy relationship with food that nourishes her body, mind and mood.

The major social and health challenges that my clients face: Many women struggle with negative thinking about what they should eat and what they should look like. They dislike and are disconnected from their bodies. Women in our culture are taught to deprive themselves, to shrink and not take up space. In my program, women become empowered to be in, listen to and enjoy their bodies. As a result, they discover themselves. They learn to speak up and ask for what they want.

What my clients love about my program: They get results, and they don't feel deprived.

My favorite juicy question to ask my clients is: What is most important to you?

The top three results my clients get from working with me are: becoming empowered to listen to and enjoy their bodies, learning a new way of eating to feel enriched and demystifying their kitchens. They get awesome physical results, too: regular periods, regular digestion, sound sleep and reduced allergy symptoms.

In addition to one-on-one counseling, I also: support my clients to find a better relationship to food and their body using the tools of emotional counseling, yoga and meditation.

What I love about what I do: being creative, seeing my clients thrive, and creating the life I want while helping others do the same thing. This work keeps challenging me to grow. Each day I am granted the opportunity to do something good for myself and others.

My greatest success so far: expanding my business. I have so much business that I've hired another health counselor to see clients with me. I've worked with hundreds of people privately and through Integrative Nutrition, and each of those people has influenced families, partners and friends. Fruition is a movement in the way women think about their health. This ripple effect is my greatest success.

In the future, I see: many Fruition Women's Health Centers around the country. This country needs new, fresh ideas and practical new approaches to how we look at food. I will also provide an awesome place for future Integrative Nutrition graduates to do the work they want to do in the world. And I see myself doing lots of yoga, walking in the woods and singing with my husband.

CLIENT TESTIMONIAL

Susan

43 | cell biologist | San Francisco, CA

I've been in the oncology field for 15 years. I have a PhD in neuroscience, and I work for a biotech company trying to put out new cancer therapeutics. I'm an avid runner, and I have a great family—my husband and two boys, aged 11 and 13. I was anorexic in high school. As an adult I've been a normal weight, but with anorexic behaviors. I was hyper-controlling and afraid of food. I wouldn't eat in front of people at parties or business meetings, and I ate only certain "safe foods". My body felt weak and withered.

Darshana was the one who helped me to enjoy food. She actually showed me how to eat; she didn't just tell me food content. She showed me how to go to the grocery store and what foods go well together. She introduced me to foods I'd never heard of and gave me lots of recipes. Our private sessions focused on calming me down and connecting me with my body.

Today my relationship with food and my body is totally different. I've lost the part of anorexia that makes me afraid of what I put in my mouth. I understand the connection between getting proper food and enjoying life. I eat high nutrition foods, feel stronger and look younger. I've run a half-marathon and climbed a 14,000-foot mountain with crampons and ice picks. My body feels strong, full and sturdy. Being anorexic, I felt isolated from the world and didn't want to interact with it. Darshana showed me that the world is a safe place.

Robert Notter

Class of 2004 | New York, NY

*It may be that the satisfaction I
need depends on my going away, so
that when I've gone and come back,
I'll find it at home. -Rumi*

Job before Integrative Nutrition: manager and analyst in technology
Childhood ambition: to be a veterinarian
Favorite snack food: cinnamon rolls
Favorite healthy food: hummus and olives
Favorite nutrition book: *Nourishing Wisdom* by Marc David, MA
Favorite exercise: dancing
Favorite activity outside of work: listening to music
What I do to treat myself: massage and travel
What I do to feel at peace: listen to meditation CDs or play with my cat
Wildest dream: saving the world from evil demons and mass destruction
Proudest moment: sitting on the airplane on my way to move to New York City
Biggest challenge: learning to turn off my mind and just be still
Health concern that I've cleared up: headaches
What I love about Integrative Nutrition: being part of a group of amazing
people, who are all on a path of love and positive change
What I love about being a health counselor: seeing others gain clarity about
their lives, face their fears and learn to be happy with who they are
What I love about my star client, Mark: his willingness to learn, grow and try
new things, and his wonderfully creative mind

ABOUT MY PRACTICE

Whole Life Institute | robert@wholelifehealing.org | www.wholelifehealing.org

My counseling specialty is: working with gay men who are interested in feeling better, loving themselves as they are and creating healthy, supportive relationships.

My typical client is: a gay man in his 30s or 40s who wants to reduce his stress and learn to like himself just as he is, without comparison to his peers or gay stereotypes.

The major social and health challenges that my clients face are: They often grew up without support, approval or appropriate role models. Many are stressed out, struggling with low self-esteem, lonely and looking for fulfilling relationships. I support them to let go of their negative thinking, while learning to love and approve of themselves unconditionally. I also address their health concerns, which include anxiety, depression, stress, irritable bowel syndrome, acid reflux, hypoglycemia, diabetes and immune system disorders like HIV.

What my clients love about my program: I tell them the truth. I am compassionate but direct, and I allow them to be just as they are, while working on reaching their personal goals. Clients like working with me because I exemplify what I teach. I treat myself well, while also being human. Having grown up gay in a small town, I know what it's like to feel unsupported and judged. I also know how healing it is to find real support, like I did at Integrative Nutrition.

My favorite juicy question to ask my clients is: Who or what is truly causing your pain?

The top three results my clients get from working with me are: realizing unhealthy patterns in their lives, taking control of their compulsive and anxiety-driven thoughts and realizing that true happiness comes from the inside, not from the external world. Everyone I work with gets better. They sleep more soundly and worry less, have more energy, rely less on caffeine and sugar, heal digestive issues, stabilize their blood sugar and strengthen their immune systems. They often reduce or wean themselves off medications like insulin and antidepressants.

In addition to one-on-one counseling, I also: teach corporate and community workshops for organizations like the Gay Men's Health Crisis Center, the LGBT Community Center and the Out Professionals business network. I also provide group counseling programs, workshops, Reiki energy healing and Pilates exercise instruction.

What I love about what I do: It is incredibly rewarding to see my clients reach their goals, learn to finally be happy and, most importantly, accept themselves for who they are. I am honored to be a guide for my clients and grateful to have the opportunity to take part in their growth.

My greatest success so far: leaving my corporate job and fully supporting myself with my private practice, while being recognized by my community as a resource for healing and health.

In the future, I see myself: reaching many parts of the world through writing, public speaking and group events. I see myself as a catalyst for positive change in the gay community, towards unity and greater acceptance of self and others.

CLIENT TESTIMONIAL

Mark
55 | writer and director | New York, NY

I work in theater, writing and directing musical comedies on Broadway. This work is my love. I've been doing it for 30 years and am very fortunate to be successful in my chosen field. One of my very popular shows finished a four-year run and left me exhausted. My health and diet had deteriorated, and I had become addicted to candy. I was eating Starburst in vast quantities. I had never had an issue with my weight, but suddenly I was 20 pounds overweight. I didn't have any energy anymore—I was completely exhausted all the time. When the show closed I had some time off to invest in my health. That's when Robert entered my life.

I like healthy food but had lost track of it. Robert reintroduced me to a way to eating that made me feel a lot better. I started eating more whole grains and beans, and lots of greens and organic produce. I also got back in touch with cooking my own food. Robert also worked with me on my breathing. New York, and especially the entertainment industry, is such a high-stress environment. Being aware of my breath and doing simple exercises in the morning helped tremendously. I also realized that exercise is crucial to my physical and mental well-being. Over about 10 months, I lost the 20 pounds.

When I met Robert I really was not feeling good, but now I am feeling terrific. I feel like I'm a better person—more equipped to deal with others because I feel better about myself. I'm grateful to Robert for introducing me to this healthy lifestyle. He was the perfect coach at the perfect time. And as we say in the theater, timing is everything!

10

Corporate Wellness

The workers of America are a mighty force. They labor to succeed and achieve grand feats. American businesses thrive because of their tremendous ambition and dedication. Yet many workers suffer from poor health and are stressed out, overweight and fatigued. They live on fast food, vending machine snacks, coffee and cigarettes. They sit all day at their desks and all night in front of their televisions. Still they toil and still American business remains strong. Imagine, then, what our workers' lives and our economy would look like if these diligent individuals were healthy and energized, if they went to work each morning fresh and excited to be alive.

Thousands of companies are visualizing just that and beginning to take action to alter the American workplace so that these dreams may transform into reality. When small businesses, universities and major corporations like Merrill Lynch and BMW invest in programs that teach employees about exercise, nutrition and stress management, their workers respond. They lose weight and take fewer sick days, and health insurance claims drop by almost 20%. There is no denying the proof in the numbers: wellness services are good for business.

The next group of profiles features Integrative Nutrition graduates who are working in corporate wellness. They were successful, productive employees who came to our school because they wanted to improve their health and use their talents to accomplish meaningful goals. They tailor their programs to achievers like themselves, and are paid top dollar to share their knowledge with high-profile companies and government agencies. They know that where American business leads, the rest of our culture tends to follow, and so as they make a difference in one company and then the next, the effects of their work reverberate, the health of our country grows, and ever greater achievements become possible.

Cheryl Mirabella-Caldwell

Class of 2004 | Alexandria, VA

Dreams are renewable. No matter what our age or condition, there are still untapped possibilities within us, and new beauty waiting to be born.

—Dale Turner

Job before Integrative Nutrition: running my own company matching human resource trainers and management consultants with a variety of companies
Childhood ambition: to run my own business
Favorite snack food: apples and peanut butter
Favorite healthy food: greens with pine nuts and dried cranberries
Favorite nutrition book: *Eating Well for Optimum Health* by Andrew Weil, MD
Favorite exercise: walking
Favorite activity outside of work: spending time with my family and friends and cooking yummy meals for those I love
Favorite vacation spot: Rome
Craziest thing I've ever done: commuted to California once a month for two years to get my master's degree
Wildest dream: to become a philanthropist, able to give easily to worthwhile causes such as the environment, healthy food and feeding children worldwide
Proudest moment: becoming a mother
Biggest challenge: balancing work and family
Health concerns I've cleared up: weight issues and sugar cravings
What I love about Integrative Nutrition: Everything! A wonderful education, incredible instructors—the support was beyond belief on every level.
What I love about being a health counselor: creating healthier and happier individuals, families and companies. There is no better feeling.
What I love about my star client, Larissa: She understands that wellness education can create a healthier and happier workforce and save companies money in healthcare costs as well.

ABOUT MY PRACTICE

Living Whole Health | cmirabella@earthlink.net | www.livingwholehealth.com

My counseling specialty is: helping clients look at how all areas of their lives impact their optimal health and energy levels, and create balance.

My typical client is: anyone who wants more energy, is ready to fall in love with healthy food and wants to live a long and exciting life. My corporate clients are big DC organizations like the Nuclear Energy Institute, the Pharmaceutical Manufacturer Representatives of America, the US Department of Agriculture, the Association of Trial Lawyers, the State Department Federal Credit Union and the Australian Embassy.

The top three results my clients get from working with me are: more energy, falling in love with healthy whole food and understanding how all areas of their lives have an impact on their health.

What my clients love about my program: With a master's degree in spiritual psychology, I take my clients down a path of inner work. We explore what their lives are about for them, and how being satisfied on all levels—mental, emotional and spiritual as well as physical—creates optimal health.

My favorite juicy question to ask my clients: If money were not an issue, what would you be doing with your life?

In addition to one-on-one counseling, I also: teach cooking classes and conduct women's wellness weekends. On the corporate level I use my contacts as a human resources broker to market wellness classes to businesses and government agencies.

What I love about what I do: I love to educate and inspire. Nothing gets me more excited than seeing people apply something they have discovered in a session or class to make life more enjoyable for themselves and those they love. I know that the world is better because of the work I do, and that is huge for me. I feel fortunate that I have found a way to make a living doing what I love.

Why I work with corporations: I am trying to change how companies think about wellness education. Human resources offices spend big money training their employees on management, technology and even stress management. But if a manager is drinking coffee and eating donuts and has an afternoon sugar crash and yells at his staff, what difference does that training make? It doesn't address the fundamental biological problem. There is also the importance of preventative care. If just one employee does not get heart disease or diabetes as a result of our talks, the company is saved thousands of dollars in healthcare costs. When I offer a high-quality program and am clear about its value, a company begins to understand the importance of investing resources in it.

My greatest success so far: developing and delivering my Wellness Series. Since 2003 I have delivered over 50 paid programs on many workplace health topics. Participants give us great feedback and say they feel fortunate to work at a company that offers this level of wellness education.

In the future, I see myself: making an even bigger impact. I would love to write a book and travel, speaking to larger audiences around the world on wellness, and eventually become a philanthropist supporting others in their healing work. I would love to see other health counselors running corporate programs like mine in their own cities. Corporate wellness initiatives are so important if we are going to change corporate culture and improve the health of working Americans.

CLIENT TESTIMONIAL

Larissa

35 | human resources manager | Washington, DC

As the HR manager for the Australian Embassy, I hired Cheryl to do wellness training for our staff. The embassy is really big on work, family and personal life balance. We have a lot of military personnel who are very into health and fitness. Other employees are into yoga or relaxation. So we are always looking out for programs that fit these interests.

Cheryl taught two series of 10 wellness programs. She tailored them to meet our staff's specific needs, which was really great. Her talks were always very well-prepared. There were presentations, discussions and cooking demonstrations. She was very calm and personable and had all the answers to all our questions. She was able to really connect with people and help them get involved in the class. She set us up with goals and a buddy system, so that we would have support and make progress from week to week.

By the end of Cheryl's program people's food choices were really different. You could see it just by looking around the room at what they were bringing in. A lot of people reported weight loss. Others went off extreme diets and introduced smaller changes that would last longer. People changed how they cooked and shopped and learned about how their bodies reacted to food. They compared what they were cutting out of their diets, like sugar or caffeine, and discussed how it affected them. They worked together on coming up with strategies for having good energy for work at different times of the day. It was great. Cheryl's was our most successful wellness training program ever. Everybody really liked it. It was definitely worthwhile—an added benefit to our staff, and an inexpensive way to increase wellness and productiveness in the office.

Christi Lehner Collins

Class of 2003 | Boston, MA

Everything and everyone prospers me now, and I prosper everyone and everything. —Catherine Ponder

Job before Integrative Nutrition: business consultant
Childhood ambition: to be an interior designer or dancer
Favorite snack food: luscious homemade trail mix of tamari-roasted almonds, pecans, dried cherries and chocolate chips
Favorite healthy food: roasted butternut squash chunks topped with caramelized agave nectar, goat cheese and pecans
Favorite nutrition book: *Women's Bodies, Women's Wisdom* by Christiane Northrup, MD
Favorite type of exercise: snowboarding, dancing, yoga or bouncing on my trampoline
Favorite activity outside of work: Saturday afternoon pentathlons with my husband, Ben—mountain biking, rollerblading, running, football and hiking— followed by a delicious dinner together
What I do to treat myself: choose something from my "nourishment menu," like relaxing with a hot water bottle, reading through old letters or cards or asking my husband to brush my hair
What I do to feel at peace: take a walk, take a shower or clear a corner of clutter
Wildest dream: to open a wellness center with a group of amazing practitioners or to live in the mountains where I can walk out the door and be immediately immersed in nature
Proudest moment: giving birth to my child
Biggest challenge: letting go, trusting, going with the flow and being gentle with myself
Health concerns I've cleared up: irritable bowel syndrome, PMS, acne, constipation and an obsessive diet mentality
What I love about Integrative Nutrition: I learned how to listen to my mind and soul to find out what I truly want to go after.
What I love about being a health counselor: watching people fall in love with healthy living in a joyous, freeing way
What I love about my star client, Fiona: So committed, so blossoming!

ABOUT MY PRACTICE

Boston Health Coach | christi@bostonhealthcoach.com | www.bostonhealthcoach.com

My counseling specialty is: inspiring busy professionals to fall in love with healthy eating, juicy living and guilt-free self-care. I have a knack for helping people see how the very ailments that annoy them the most (and that haven't responded well to traditional medical treatments) are actually very important messengers sent by their bodies to get them to slow down and take care of themselves. I have had great success supporting clients to heal irritable bowel syndrome, hypoglycemia and low energy.

My typical client is: a successful corporate professional who is extremely driven, perfectionistic, intellectually curious and educated about "traditional nutrition." Their own health has been bumped to the bottom of their priority list. As a result, they are exhausted, tough on themselves and tired of eating restrictive diets and living boring lives.

The top three results my clients get from working with me are: figuring out what they really want out of life; learning to love themselves, honor their needs, and speak up for what they want without feeling guilty; and healing physical and emotional ailments that have been hanging around for years.

What my clients love about my program: They say goodbye to beliefs and habits that were holding them back—like an obsessive diet mentality, a poor self-image, fear of the unknown or negative self-talk—and free up that energy to focus on something that makes them feel truly alive.

My favorite juicy question to ask my clients is: If you only had until the end of the week to live, how would you want to spend your last week?

In addition to one-on-one counseling, I also: lead monthly teleclasses and live seminars for large corporations like Deloitte, Hewlett-Packard, the US Postal Service, Eaton Vance, as well as for hospitals and schools. I write and publish articles, books and an online nutrition program for marathon runners and provide business training to other health counselors. I recently produced my first DVD, called *Healthy Shopper*.

Why I work with corporations: I used to be a strategic management consultant, which is about as much fun as it sounds. The stress aggravated my irritable bowel syndrome, and I suffered through every workday in pain. Integrative Nutrition took me on the journey of healing my stomach. The school also gave me a blueprint for using the success I had in my corporate job to help others feel better. It's my goal to inspire business professionals to lead the way towards a business environment that will allow them to do their best work and stay healthy at the same time.

What I love about what I do: I have the power to create the kind of work schedule and structure that supports my needs and lifestyle. I love expanding health counseling into so many different income sources—speaking, writing, counseling, TV work, business coaching, etc. The possibilities are endless.

My greatest success so far: having so many people decide to attend Integrative Nutrition after working with me, attending one of my seminars or reading my newsletter. Knowing that the world has more health counselors because of the connections I've made and the work I've done is so inspiring.

In the future, I see myself: creating a welcoming, gorgeous wellness center that brings together a fabulous community of practitioners to support women, and continuing to facilitate teleclasses and seminars for corporations.

CLIENT TESTIMONIAL

Fiona

42 | fashion industry expert-turned-mom | Swampscott, MA

I'm originally from the UK, and spent 20 years in the fashion industry. I worked in the design and technical sides of the business and loved the creativity, the travel and working with people all around the world. Today I am a stay-at-home mom with two gorgeous little boys. When I met Christi I had been diagnosed with celiac disease. The symptoms were terrible. I had energy highs and lows, bad migraines, bloating, constipation, sinus problems and fatigue. I was also focusing all my time and attention on others and my needs weren't getting met. I very quickly realized that I needed Christi's help.

Christi is very positive and extremely smart. She added exciting, colorful foods to my diet and taught me about grains that I could digest and that made me feel good. My energy level increased, my digestion calmed down and my constipation cleared up. We also made time for my personal desires including painting, meditation, journaling, exercise and a wardrobe makeover. Once I started to do some of those things, I couldn't believe how much better I felt.

I used to feel selfish for taking time out for myself, but Christi helped me realize that taking care of myself makes me a better role model for my children. When I feel happy and healthy, so do they. Christi is an amazing coach. I'm so grateful to her for changing my life in this positive way and making me the happiest person I've been in 42 years!

Charles Berg
DC

Class of 2005 | Ridgewood, NJ

Cages are cages whether constructed of steel and concrete or from the fabric of the mind. The mind sets the limits of bondage and provides the gate to liberty.

-Gerry Spence

Job: doctor of chiropractic
Childhood ambition: to be a professional baseball player
Favorite snack food: Goobers Peanuts
Favorite healthy food: trail mix
Favorite nutrition book: *Nourishing Wisdom* by Marc David, MA
Favorite exercise: swimming or playing racquetball
Favorite activity outside of work: public speaking
What I do to treat myself: play my drums
What I do to feel at peace: read spiritual books, especially in the woods
Wildest dream: reaching audiences around the world
Proudest moment: speaking to an audience of 900 people at New York Chiropractic College
Biggest challenge: learning to live in the moment
Health concerns I've cleared up: digestive bloating and distention (by eliminating most dairy and sugar)
What I love about Integrative Nutrition: learning about the impact of primary foods on our total health
What I love about being a health counselor: the opportunity to facilitate change in people's lives
What I love about my star client, Jeff: watching someone take total personal responsibility for his life

ABOUT MY PRACTICE

Transformational Lifestyle Management/River Vale Chiropractic Center |
chiroman123@aol.com | www.DrChuckBerg.com

My counseling specialty is: helping my clients chunk life down into manageable days and balance the physical, emotional, mental and spiritual arenas.

My typical client is: most often a "baby boomer" who wants to reduce stress, lose weight and reengineer his or her lifestyle.

What my clients love about my program: my clear, concise, serene support and how I always make them feel that their goals are attainable. I help them look at their belief systems and values—that is, what generates their motivation to heal. I strive to share honestly about my own life and support them wherever they are in their process, without judgment.

The top three results my clients get from working with me are: clarity, an understanding of food and its impact on the body, and the confidence to face fears rather than to hide from them.

My favorite juicy question to ask my clients is: If there were no possibility of failure, what would you do?

In addition to one-on-one counseling, I also: facilitate wellness seminars for large corporations. I have also been a successful chiropractor for the past 28 years, consulting daily with patients about their health issues and being a loving, guiding presence in their lives.

What I love about what I do: Supporting others provides me with both success and significance. By doing what my heart yearns to do, I feel energized every day.

Why I work with corporations: Corporate culture is starting to understand that a company is only as good as the individuals who work there. I teach corporate employees about conscious eating, stress management and the structure and function of the body. I believe that unless our country develops a new understanding of health now, future generations will be trapped in unhealthy habits and environments, too. As a father, I want our next generations to be healthy.

My greatest success so far: being hired to teach my wellness program to big companies like BMW of North America and other multibillion dollar corporations that understand the importance of wellness education.

In the future, I see myself: lecturing around the world at major venues for Fortune 500 companies, teaching seminars on cruise ships and making the world my classroom.

CLIENT TESTIMONIAL

Jeff

47 | operations manager | Edison, NJ

I'm the head of operations for a Japanese manufacturing company, and I'm very committed to my family, so I work hard to keep life in balance. I'm married to my best friend and high school sweetheart, and we have two beautiful teenage daughters. I feel blessed to have a great life. I met Dr. Berg 25 years ago when I was a bad boy, alcoholic and drug addict. I was in a car accident and went to him for chiropractic care. For years I've gone to him for two types of adjustment—the spine and the attitude.

About a year ago I signed up for his nutrition program. As part of being in recovery, I was running marathons and eating just about anything. I was overindulging in carbohydrates and sweets, and then burning them off in training. Physically I looked okay, but internally I wasn't. With Dr. Berg I learned to eat better. Now I love fish, chicken and every vegetable. I don't add salt to anything. I eat small portions of pasta because I still need it for my activity level. Eating these foods makes me feel cleaner. It has made me more vibrant and put a spring in my step.

Since working with Dr. Berg my whole life has improved. I'm more involved with my church and other organizations, and I'm into giving, sharing and caring, not just going through life asleep. I really can't say enough good things about Dr. Berg. He is a very caring individual. I'm grateful to him for always being there for me and for being so encouraging.

11

Reaching the Globe

W e live in an era of communication. Modern technology has made possible swift, clear connection across the world. Boundaries of physical distance have been superceded, and we have the opportunity to link across international lines, to experience our inherent oneness with other peoples and communities everywhere.

Sadly, one consequence of this globalization is that the ill health of Americans, fueled by our hectic lifestyles and fast-food fanaticism, has spread to other lands. McDonald's and Dunkin' Donuts have swept the globe, and with them heart disease, obesity and other illnesses.

Integrative Nutrition is working to reverse this trend, spreading our message of health and well-being throughout the world as well. Our health counselors are working in Asia, Europe, and North and South Americas. Some alumni travel regularly and have client bases in multiple countries. We have students from the Caribbean, Africa, Scandinavia, Canada and Australia. This is only the beginning.

The health counselors in this chapter are serving as ambassadors. Living in and visiting foreign lands, they are teaching the simple values of positive lifestyle changes and eating wholesome, locally grown foods. Their work reinforces the ways in which we are all interlinked. As our great country becomes healthier and happier, so too will the rest of our planet.

Ana Rocha

Class of 2004 | Miami Beach, FL

Let your food be your medicine,
and your medicine be your food.

—Hippocrates

Job before Integrative Nutrition: lawyer in Brazil, finance professional in the US
Childhood ambition: to be successful
Favorite snack food: chocolate
Favorite healthy food: broccoli, arugula or fruit
Favorite kitchen tool: the food!
Favorite exercise: running
Favorite activity outside of work: going to the beach
Favorite vacation spot: Buenos Aires or Madrid
Craziest thing I've ever done: go to New York City in the winter
(I hate cold weather!)
Other cities I've lived in: Rio de Janeiro, Brazil, and San Francisco, CA
Wildest dream: to own a beautiful spa
Proudest moment: when a client finishes my program and is thrilled with
the results
Health concerns I've cleared up: mid-day chocolate cravings
What I love about Integrative Nutrition: everything I learned there
What I love about being a health counselor: working with food and helping my
clients live better, healthier lives
What I love about my star client, Isabel: her willpower to achieve her goal, and
how happy she was with her results

ABOUT MY PRACTICE

Ana Rocha, Holistic Nutritionist | anac_rocha@yahoo.com | www.nutritionspa.net

My counseling specialties are: weight loss, exercise and teaching about food and nutrition. Sometimes people find healthy food boring. I teach them how to cook, to vary their food, and to find healthier alternatives according to their tastes.

My typical client is: already health-conscious, but wants to lose weight and improve their health even more. I have a lot of foreign clients. I do nutritional counseling in Portuguese, Spanish and English, and I have a collection of healthy recipes in all three languages. I have clients in Brazil and Colombia, and I work with many Latin people here in the US.

The top three results my clients get from working with me are: weight loss, eating better and regular exercise—a recipe for a better life! I work with them for three to six months, and they totally meet their goals. They feel happier and more energized because they have learned how to make the best out of healthy eating.

What my clients love about my program: They learn new things about food and nutrition, like how to shop more effectively, how to cook healthy food, new and delicious recipes, and how to improve their families' eating habits. People choose me as their counselor because of the passion that I have for nutrition.

My favorite juicy question to ask my clients: What's your goal and why?

In addition to one-on-one counseling, I also: teach workshops and cooking classes. My business partner and I have a small clinic where I do nutritional counseling and she does skin treatments. I take care of the inside, and she takes care of the outside! We also offer yoga instruction and are growing to include a massage therapist and other practitioners.

What I love about what I do: I love working with food because I truly believe that "you are what you eat"—physically and emotionally. I think health is the most important thing in life. If it's missing, you can't really do anything else that you love.

Why I work internationally: I like being around people from everywhere. I especially like to work with clients in Brazil. People there are more health conscious than people in the U.S. I am from Rio, a beach city where people work out, and where there's no junk food or fast-food culture. Even the sandwiches are healthier. When Latin people come to the US, you can see how their eating habits change from when they were kids. Sometimes they gain weight or develop other health problems when they come here. I can help them with that.

My greatest success so far: Leaving my job to start my own business as a health counselor. I always wanted to have more freedom in my career, to do something for myself that I love. Now I have more time to go back to Brazil and see family and friends. It's awesome!

In the future, I see: lots of happy, healthy people who've done my program!

CLIENT TESTIMONIAL

Isabel

40 | yoga instructor | Miami, FL

I own my own yoga studio, and I am married with two kids, two and four years old. I am committed to my career and to taking care of my family's health and happiness, and my own. I was looking for someone to help me improve my own and my family's diets. I was eating healthily but didn't have much time or energy to cook. I'm very busy and sometimes don't have time for myself. I needed someone to help me find time to exercise and to lose a few extra pounds. I also wanted to learn more about organic food and how to balance my diet well.

I have a friend who worked with Ana and had great results. I knew immediately that Ana would be great to work with. She's very professional, committed and concerned for her clients' health. Plus, she's a good example—she's fit, eats well and takes care of herself. Ana taught me better ways to shop for food, and how to prepare delicious meals. Eating better has improved my mental and physical health, as well as my family's. Even though I teach yoga, I wasn't getting my exercise done. Ana helped me to get organized and to find time to exercise more often. I even learned to take time for myself. And I lost the extra pounds I wanted to lose.

I so appreciate Ana for never allowing me to give up. She always pushed me to achieve my goals and was always there for me. She is passionate about what she does, and she shows it! She was an inspiration. I am very happy I found her.

Joyce Kempis Marot

Class of 2005 | Hong Kong, China

There came a time when staying tight within the bud became more painful than the strain it took to blossom.
—Anaïs Nin

Job before Integrative Nutrition: personal trainer, health and fitness model and writer

Childhood ambition: to be an ambassador

Favorite snack food: dark chocolate—Valrohna 85% or Lindt 99%

Favorite healthy food: apples and bananas with raw almond butter

Favorite nutrition book: *Conscious Eating* by Gabriel Cousens, MD

Favorite exercise: weight training, yoga or running

Favorite activity outside of work: spending time with my loved ones and reading

What I do to treat myself: fly on a whim to anyplace in the world with sunshine and white sandy beaches

Other cities I've lived in: Los Angeles, CA; Hanover, Germany; Cancun, Mexico; Jakarta, Indonesia; and Avignon, France (to name a few)

Wildest dream: to open a holistic health and healing center in St. Barth's. My daily uniform would be a bikini, a sarong and fancy-free footwear.

Proudest moment: the day I got married to a wonderful man. (We married after knowing each other for only three weeks, and after being married for 15 years, we are still madly in love.)

Biggest challenge: being a pack rat

Health concerns I've cleared up: extreme cravings for sweets and chocolate

What I love about Integrative Nutrition: It speaks the truth, shares its wisdom, and heals, supports, loves and nourishes everyone who becomes a part of its community.

What I love about being a health counselor: truly making a difference in someone's life in just one day

What I love about my star client, Daniela: She's resilient, open, adventurous and tremendously fun to work with.

ABOUT MY PRACTICE

Health Euphoria | healthiswealth@musclemessiah.com | www.health-euphoria.com

My counseling specialty is: health, healing and wholeness through exercise, personalized nutrition and nourishment. I help my clients build mental muscles to live optimally and abundantly.

My typical clients are: individuals looking to balance their personal and professional lives. They are seeking guidance and support to help them commit to exercising, eating healthy and leading a more balanced life.

The top three results my clients get from working with me are: increased energy, fitness level and sense of well-being. They also clear up problems with cravings, bingeing, weight gain and emotional eating, so they feel less stuck and more balanced.

My favorite juicy question to ask my clients is: What was the first thought you had when you woke up this morning?

What my clients love about my program: It's innovative, fun, engaging and always fresh and new. Beyond diet and exercise, we address finding ways to be of service to others, be creative, revisit lost dreams, and get back to having full, balanced lives. My clients tell me they feel very listened to and supported.

In addition to one-on-one counseling, I also: do personal training, write health and fitness articles, organize workshops and lectures and do product promotions. I am also the nutrition consultant for the first-ever vegan restaurant in Hong Kong, which opened last year.

What I love about what I do: It's not work, it's love. I'm passionate about giving people life and vitality. Every day I learn something new that allows me to grow.

What it was like attending Integrative Nutrition from Asia: I've had a really exciting life, and I love to travel. I've lived in many different parts of the world, like Mexico, the Bahamas and Indonesia. I'm married to a Frenchman and together we divide our time between Hong Kong, the south of France and California. One day I was visiting New York City, and I walked into a health food restaurant. I saw the Integrative Nutrition catalog, and it sang to me. I wasn't going to move to the States, so for each class weekend I made the 18-hour flight from Hong Kong to New York. It was wonderful—just a matter of getting focused on what I really wanted—and my business was enhanced overnight.

My greatest success so far: increasing my income by 100 percent when I decided that I wanted more prosperity in my life. The power of intention has worked for me ever since.

In the future, I see myself: reaching more people from different parts of the world, educating and inspiring them to lead healthier and happier lives. I will also be developing programs for media and entertainment to spread the knowledge about health and wellness.

CLIENT TESTIMONIAL

Daniela

40 | hospitality executive | State of Qatar

I have been a typical busy executive for many years, carrying many responsibilities and always going through new challenges. I work in the tourism and hospitality industry and travel frequently, which I like very much. Joyce was my personal trainer when I lived in Hong Kong. I was going through an emotionally difficult time, and she was a tremendous support.

Joyce helped me to adapt my fitness routine based on what I was going through, since my emotional state impacted my body as well. It was important for me to learn how to eat food that would make me feel good, since I was emotionally low. Another counselor was trying to prescribe antidepressants for me, but with Joyce I was able to eat the right type of food to make me feel better. I truly learned to look at food differently and to experiment with grains, vegetables and protein. I learned more about sugar and how to keep my energy going through the day without putting my body through ups and downs. Now I never have cravings. My shape totally changed for the better. I reduced body fat and became leaner. I dropped a dress size and have kept my new shape for over a year.

Now I no longer diet or sacrifice. My mood is balanced, and I've really learned how to care for myself. My body really does speak to me, and I can feel what is right for me or not. I am so grateful that Joyce was there when I needed her most. Now that I have moved from Hong Kong to Qatar, what I learned from her still helps me every single day.

Mary Kent Hearon

Class of 2002 | London, England and the US

When you want something, all the world conspires in helping you to achieve it.
                                    -Paulo Coelho

Job before Integrative Nutrition: director of operations at a venture capital firm
Childhood ambition: to be an entrepreneur
Favorite snack food: rice cakes with manuka honey and almond butter
Favorite healthy food: sautéed kale with olive oil and garlic
Favorite kitchen tool: my OXO carrot peeler
Favorite exercise: kickboxing or Pilates
Favorite activity outside of work: walking in the park
Other cities I've lived in: New York, Columbia, SC, and Paris
Craziest thing I've ever done: moved to London to start a business
Wildest dream: having a television show
Proudest moment: when I graduated from Integrative Nutrition
Biggest challenge: starting my newsletter and my business
Health concerns I've cleared up: sinus problems, weakened immune system, antibiotic overload, repeated flu, lack of energy and depression
What I love about being a health counselor: guiding clients through health transformations
What I love about Integrative Nutrition: I found myself.
What I love about my star client, Elisa: She is just like me.

ABOUT MY PRACTICE

Dragonfly Wellness™ and The Weekly Beet™ | mk@dragonflywellness.com |
www.dragonflywellness.com | www.weeklybeet.com

My counseling specialty is: educating clients to make healthy choices.

My typical client is: female and wants to lose weight. I also work with a lot of diabetics, and people who are simply interested in making healthy changes in their lives.

My favorite juicy question to ask my clients is: What is your blood type?

The top three results my clients get from working with me are: More energy, weight loss and consuming less sugar and caffeine.

What my clients love about my program: They learn to let go of their minds, listening to and trusting their bodies instead. They are attracted to working with me because I truly walk my talk, and I help them get amazing results.

In addition to one-on-one counseling, I also: started a hip, educational newsletter called *The Weekly Beet*. It has become hugely popular, with over 4,000 readers. I was invited by a producer in the UK to turn it into a television program, so I moved my practice to London where I am developing the show. Being overseas means I'm doing more online, international counseling, which I find really exciting! Most recently I have partnered up with Elisa Rusconi to start Nutrishionista™, a six-month program of complete nutrition and fashion transformation.

How I got started in health counseling: I worked with cardiac patients at Columbia Cardiology Consultants in my hometown in South Carolina. I began by teaching lectures and writing pamphlets about cholesterol, diabetes, blood pressure and weight loss. Then I began counseling patients, and their health results were so incredible that doctors invited me to be their in-house nutritionist—the first ever in a doctor's office in my town. People loved it!

What I love about what I do: I have created the life I have always dreamed of. Every single talent I possess has been uncovered since the day I signed up for the course at Integrative Nutrition. Writing about the truth in the health industry is extremely rewarding. Spreading the word about new organic products through *The Weekly Beet*™ is so much fun. Also, educating people on the importance of eating right is an incredible feeling!

My greatest success so far: I authored a book called *Columbia's Essential Guide To Weight Loss*, which is a dietary journal for the people of Columbia with information about healthy stores and restaurants in the city, diet, sugar, caffeine and more. It's a big hit there. I give it to my clients, and I'm working to get versions published for different cities across the United States. I have been featured in *Vogue UK* and *Elle*.

In the future, I see myself: lecturing more and writing books. My role is to share the gift that was given to me at Integrative Nutrition: truthful knowledge about healing the body. I will forever be coming up with new ways to get that message out to the world, through media, Internet or face-to face-connections.

CLIENT TESTIMONIAL

Elisa

32 | health writer and editor | London, UK

I used to work as a public relations manager and fashion journalist in Europe. Then I came down with a terrible form of facial eczema as well as serious digestive problems. I went to the best conventional doctors in Italy and underwent all sorts of analysis and exams. No one was able to identify the real cause of my eczema—that I was very stressed, and my body was sick because of my lifestyle. I drank way too much coffee and alcohol, skipped breakfast and ate a lot of fried foods, dairy and wheat. As a result I was energetically drained as well as depressed.

Mary Kent and I were great friends, and when she found out that I was unwell, she took me on board as a client. My diet changed drastically. I introduced breakfast, fruits and vegetables into my diet. I stopped skipping meals and eliminated dairy, wheat and sugar. As a result my digestion improved and my stress levels decreased. I noticed increased energy, better moods and an overall sense of well-being. I was finally able to respect myself, listen to my body and enhance my awareness and my intuition. I created a life full of love and creativity, not stress, anger and destructive relationships, as I had before.

I left my fashion job to join Mary Kent in the production of her website, her amazing newsletter *The Weekly Beet*™, and our new business together, Nutrishionista™. Now I spread the word to help others physically in pain find release and a cure for their suffering. I love working with Mary Kent, and I want to thank her for guiding me to a path of well-being and inner happiness.

A Lifelong Career

At Integrative Nutrition we teach that everyone has a predictable future, a future that will automatically occur if one tries to fit in and follow the rules. Changing to a whole foods diet, practicing radical self-care and creating a satisfying personal life can open everyone up to greater magnificence. A higher good is achieved by setting clear intentions, working hard, believing in the self and cooperating with the beneficent universal force that wants the very best for each of us. .

Men and women who come to our school find their lives move in extraordinary directions. After graduation, ever more opportunities and assistance cross their paths. The veteran graduates who write in these next pages have found that the more they listen to and help others, the more they progress in their own lives. Their health has improved, and they have cultivated a high degree of creativity, flexibility and aliveness. The longer they counsel, the simpler and more intuitive it becomes. These graduates understand the satisfaction that comes from contributing to a mission larger than themselves. They have not lived their predictable futures; they have created lives of abundance and purpose.

We invite you to get clear about what your predictable future looks like and what exciting future you would rather have instead. Where are you holding back from designing that desired future today? Remember, this is your one, precious life. When you play small, the world cannot benefit from what you have to offer. Open your mind, open your heart and jump into a prosperous, brilliant tomorrow!

Carin McKay

Class of 1999 | San Francisco, CA

Fear is just excitement without breath. -Fritz Perls

Job before Integrative Nutrition: chef
Childhood ambition: to be an astronaut
Favorite snack food : Haigs red pepper spread with rice chips
Favorite healthy food: kale and brown rice with miso tahini sauce
Favorite nutrition book: *The Diet Cure* by Julia Ross, MA
Favorite exercise: weight lifting or dancing
Favorite activity outside of work: cooking or meditation
What I do to treat myself: go out to a great meal
What I do to feel at peace: spend time at the ocean
Wildest dream: to write three books and to teach nationally
Proudest moment: the first time I taught at Integrative Nutrition
Biggest challenge: time management and deciding what is the right thing
to do first
Health concerns I've cleared up: hypoglycemia and extra weight
What I love about Integrative Nutrition: It is one of the most innovative,
practical and life-changing experiences. It is a real education that is
truly integrated.
What I love about being a health counselor: seeing people grow and thrive
What I love about my star client, Anne: her determination to heal

ABOUT MY PRACTICE

Full Circle | carin@carinmckay.com | www.carinmckay.com

My counseling specialty is: integrating nutritional change with emotional well-being.

My typical client: tends to be in okay health, and is coming to me to experience full health in their physical, emotional and spiritual bodies. Many of my clients are activists, visionaries and people on a spiritual path. They challenge themselves to grow personally and to change the world politically, socially or environmentally. These hard-working perfectionists want to make a difference, but have overlooked basic elements of life, like nourishing themselves with good food or enjoying one-on-one relating.

The top three results my clients get from working with me are: They feel connected to their bodies and what they want. They feel free from what they "should" do and instead learn to trust their "gut." They get an outside perspective supporting them to be fully who they are. This outside perspective prevents them from repeating old patterns over and over again.

My favorite juicy questions to ask my clients are: What do you want in your life? What are your visions for yourself and others?

In addition to one-on-one counseling, I also: lead workshops and teach cooking classes. I also have a catering business. We prepare organic, natural-foods–based California cuisine.

What my clients love about my program: the connection they feel with me and the results they see in every area of their life. They love the sense of play in our sessions.

What I love about what I do: That I get to really get "in" there with a person and see what makes them tick. By getting to know what makes them tick, I get to see a person blossom into who they fully are. It's the best work in the world.

My greatest success so far: It has been a tremendous success for me to do work that I love and support myself financially. I created a practice that fully integrates all of who I am. I get to support others, have a good time and also grow, myself. I think it is a miracle that I have created a livelihood that I love.

How my life has changed: It used to be hard to find a job that fit who I was. I was on a quest to make a great livelihood in a career that was good for me and made a difference. That's when I found Integrative Nutrition. At the school I finally learned how to pair my passion for counseling with my love of food to create a successful business. When I look back over how far I've come, I am proud of myself and thankful I finally found a career that complements all of me.

In my future, I see: a center that integrates all that I do and love—food, emotional well-being, spirituality, study, interpersonal connection and community. I see a strong and thriving practice. I see myself writing three books, teaching classes around the country and being part of a movement that is about full health.

CLIENT TESTIMONIAL

Anne

30 | whole foods chef | San Francisco, CA

I am originally from Denmark and have lived in the US for 10 years. I am an organic chef and part of the Slow Food Movement. Food is my passion, but I was bulimic for 12 years. I was very good at hiding and managing my illness. When I ate, it was very healthy, organic food, but I was lethargic, dehydrated and had stomach acid in my teeth. I finally got a wake-up call and decided it was time to stop.

Carin is fantastic, and I found her at exactly the right time. She has a sense of powerful womanhood that emanates from her. Working with her saved my life on a basic level. She got me taking vitamins and minerals, and foods to help me digest them. She helped me to deal with stress and family situations and, without judgment, gave me permission to fail if I needed to. Within three weeks of working with her, my bulimic behaviors began to stop.

Today I am no longer bulimic. I eat three meals a day. My brain and body connection has healed— I am able to feel hunger and decipher what my body wants. I love butternut squash, sweet potatoes, beets, leafy greens, garlic, and organic hamburgers with blue cheese and avocado. I can relax and share a drink or a meal with the people I love. It's odd how easy it was to break the pattern, once I had someone to help me. I am grateful to Carin for saving my life, and also for supporting me to have a meaningful career working with food. I am looking forward to spreading awareness about the importance of healthy cooking and eating. Now I have the energy to do it!

Holly Anne Shelowitz

Class of 2000 | Kingston, NY

Tell me what you eat, and I will tell you what you are.
—Anthelme Brillat-Savarin

Job before Integrative Nutrition: professional photographer
Childhood ambition: to be a photographer
Favorite snack food: raw milk cheese on rye crackers
Favorite healthy food: organic grass-fed filet mignon and kale
Favorite nutrition book: *Nourishing Traditions* by Sally Fallon
Favorite exercise: hiking, walking, biking and swimming
Favorite activity outside of work: being in nature
Favorite vacation spot: my summer home on the lake
Craziest thing I've ever done: leaving my successful photography
business in the city where I'd lived for 16 years to be a health counselor
out in the country
Wildest dream: to live in the Caribbean for the winter
Proudest moment: reading an article in *New York Newsday* about the
health counseling program I did for UPS drivers, and hearing what each
driver had to say about how much I helped him
Biggest challenge: managing my time well in a busy and fulfilling life
Health concerns I've cleared up: addiction to bread and intense sweet
cravings
What I love about Integrative Nutrition: how much fun it is to learn there,
and how affirming it is about how much we already know
What I love about being a health counselor: making a difference in people's
lives in such important ways
What I love about my star client, Carrie: her joy in learning, openness to
guidance and courage to live her dreams

ABOUT MY PRACTICE

The Center for Nourishment and Healing | holly@nourishingwisdom.com | nourishingwisdom.com

My counseling specialty is: helping clients understand their cravings and nourish themselves well, and educating them about the importance of fats and proteins.

My typical clients are: women of all ages (and some brave men) who want to feel better and learn how to be healthier. Often they are on medication for high blood pressure, high cholesterol, irritable bowel syndrome or hormonal problems. If a client shows up to work with me, it's because she knows that the usual diet and medical advice isn't the whole story.

What my clients love about my program: how much better they feel right away and how as they eat more healthily, their intuition becomes highly acute. They love how living according to their true yearnings improves their overall health.

My favorite juicy question to ask my clients is: What do you crave to eat, and what do you truly crave in your life?

The top three results my clients get from working with me are: Their cravings don't run their lives anymore, they have more energy and they are well-informed about cutting-edge nutrition information. A very common result is renewed passion for life, because they feel so healthy. Clients also tell me they are relying more on their intuition to lead them to the right food, lifestyle, career and relationship choices.

In addition to one-on-one counseling, I also: lead women's groups, teach in corporations, and make and sell organic body care products. Teaching clients how to cook is a big part of my program, too. Cooking is an integral part of my own happiness and personal nurturing, so I love being in the kitchen, sharing that simple wisdom with clients.

What I love about what I do: It touches my soul like nothing else.

My greatest success so far: counseling and teaching 300 UPS drivers about health and nutrition. I've also taught at Eileen Fisher Clothing Company and had many articles written about my work.

How my life has changed: Six years ago I left a successful yet exhausting professional photography career and fulfilled my dream of moving from Manhattan to the country. Since then I've had an active counseling practice working with many, many people. Each day I cook delicious, healthy food and inspire clients to make positive changes in their lives. This work clearly makes a profound difference for others, and it also supports my own health and development. My life looks totally different now than it did seven years ago. Integrative Nutrition has made my life what it is meant to be.

In the future, I see: my loving husband, my beautiful healthy children, a satisfying, prosperous practice filled with wonderful clients, and frequent travel to the Caribbean.

CLIENT TESTIMONIAL

Carrie

32 | coordinator of Buddhist retreat center | Accord, NY

When I met Holly I was working too hard and struggling with low energy. My doctor tested me for low thyroid and anemia but, after that, could not help me. I wasn't eating well and was at the end of my rope in terms of cooking. I had an all-or-nothing approach, making either major 20 ingredient recipes or tater-tots in the oven. Because I associated cooking with stress, I didn't enjoy it. I needed inspiration, in the kitchen and in my life.

I went to Holly's cooking class and signed up as a client that same night. Her expertise about food and nutrition was obvious, and she gave everyone the feeling that cooking is not a big deal, that anyone can do it. With Holly I made connections between food, exercise, my moods and what was going on in my life. I learned the nuts and bolts of how my body works, tried new foods and learned not to let old biases limit me. My cooking has become something social, nurturing and supportive, instead of a stress. I now know how to make quick, nutritious meals. If I'm in a rush, I make kale, carrots and beans instead of tater-tots—so much more creative!

Since my work with Holly I have more energy and I am enjoying my life. People have commented on how much brighter and healthier I look, especially my skin and eyes. I've also lost weight through exercising and eating healthy fats. My menstrual cycle has improved dramatically—almost no cramps or PMS. I'm grateful to Holly for giving me a whole new set of reasons to eat and for being so loving and supportive.

Zemach Zohar

Class of 2000 | New York, NY and Israel

It is not so much that we need to be taken out of exile. It is that the exile must be taken out of us.
—Rebbe Schneerson

My job before Integrative Nutrition: advertising executive
My childhood ambition: driving a garbage truck
My favorite snack food: zapote (a delicious fruit)
My favorite healthy food: green salad decorated with seaweeds, avocado, fresh sprouts and lots of lemon
My favorite nutrition book: *Eco Eating* by Sapoty Brook
My favorite exercise: yoga
My favorite activity outside of work: traveling, spending time in nature and studying
What I do to treat myself: observe Shabbat as a full day of rest with a complete break from work—no phone, no computer
What I do to feel at peace: yoga and meals with friends
My wildest dream: de-oxymoronizing the phrase "healthy Jewish food"
My proudest moment: quitting my office job and becoming a health counselor
My biggest challenge: deciding which country to live in
What I love about Integrative Nutrition: It gave me the inspiration to set myself free from many personal and professional constraints.
Health concerns I've cleared up: extra weight
What I love about being a health counselor: actively witnessing individual lives improving and taking part in making this world a better, more delicious place
What I love about my star client, Roseanne: her optimism and trust

ABOUT MY PRACTICE

Alok Holistic Health | info@alokhealth.com | www.alokhealth.com | www.bodytemple.info

My counseling specialty is: working with artists, writers and performers.

My typical client is: dealing with a physiological or emotional blockage and wants to face it in order to heal it. They are often an urban person trying to live a healthier, more holistic life.

What my clients love about my program: the safe space, low-pressure environment, informality and warmth. They also like having their buttons pushed when needed. Many of them appreciate the supportive community I provide through group events and retreats.

The top three results my clients get from working with me are: more vitality, clearer direction with their careers and greater happiness. Their health concerns seem to simply evaporate. When I take my clients on retreats they especially begin to open up. The new environments challenge their assumptions. They begin to see more options for their health and life and to become who they really are.

My favorite juicy question to ask my clients is: Can you repeat what you've just said so you too can hear it and learn from it?

In addition to one-on-one counseling, I also: take people on adventure trips and organize events on topics that are close to my heart. More than a business, Alok Health is a community of people helping others to integrate urban lifestyles with holistic living. Other health counselors and healing practitioners work with me to offer counseling, cooking classes, lectures and meditations. I focus on our retreats to Costa Rica and the Sinai Desert and on our holistic and spiritual parties called Body Temple.

What I love about what I do: working for myself, meeting interesting people, being of service and being reminded that no matter how much I think I know, I'll always be a student of life. I view my job as simply keeping my door open for fellow travelers to peek into my life and share in my knowledge and experiences.

My greatest success so far: making a living as a health counselor. My community's high-quality Body Temple parties have also become hugely successful in the last few years. The parties bring together healers, teachers, artists, performers, DJs, chefs and others to create an environment where people can get high on great food and music, but stay in their senses and aware of themselves. It's wonderful nightlife for holistically-oriented urban people.

How my life has changed: I had a job in advertising working on big corporate and government accounts. I would refuse to work on fast food accounts and army contracts because they didn't fit my values. I would have business meetings with Congress members, and then days later be in the street demonstrating against them. Integrative Nutrition's main message to me was to live my own life. By becoming a health counselor I've connected with and become a bridge for many remarkable, creative and healing people. I love being part of something bigger than just myself. This is my career now, and it's amazing.

In the future, I see myself: helping to bring nutritional and spiritual awareness to important institutions like hospitals, schools, religious institutions and even the army and the police.

CLIENT TESTIMONIAL

Roseanne

30 | actor and health counselor | New York, NY

In 2001 I was a fledgling actor looking for jobs in the city, working as a legal secretary to pay the bills and hating every second of it. Fortunately, I met my partner, Frankie, at the law firm. Frankie is Dominican and a great cook, and I gained 15 pounds in the first month of our relationship. I needed to figure out how I could lose weight, eat healthier and stay in my relationship.

Zemach was a great counselor. I would walk into our sessions not knowing what to talk about and walk out feeling lighter, happier and full of possibilities. In his cooking classes I learned how to cook with confidence, creativity and spontaneity, and found that preparing my own food is the most healthful way for me. I learned to cook vegetables, reduced animal foods and sugar and added healthy fats to my diet. I lost the extra 15 pounds in three months. My hair, skin and nails improved, and I cleared up my PMS, cramps and hormonal rashes. It was amazing.

Frankie supported my transition into healthy eating, and today he is eating more healthfully too. Zemach helped me to improve my relationship skills; I learned not to be dogmatic—about food or about love. Through Zemach I also learned about Integrative Nutrition. Today I have a permanent stage-acting job in a great show, and I see clients part-time. I make plenty of money, I don't work too hard and I love both my jobs. Today I'm a health counselor, but I was a client first, so I know that this approach works!

Index of Graduates

You can find out about more successful Integrative Nutrition graduates in our Online Graduate Directory. Just visit www.integrativenutrition.com to search for a graduate by location or health counseling specialty.